1/25/2

Happy Birthday

Will —

Bri

GORDON SUTHERLAND: DAMN YOU FAT FINGERS

BEST TYPING MISTAKES AND AUTOCORRECT FAILS

GORDON SUTHERLANDs
# DAMN YOU
BEST TYPING MISTAKES AND AUTOCORRECT FAILS
# FAT FINGERS

ISBN-13: 978-1500850883
ISBN-10: 1500850888

New eBook Media Ltd.
Company Number 8802144

Book Website & Contact
www.facebook.com/damnyoufatfingers

Give feedback on the book at:
damnyoufatfingers@gmail.com

Printed in
U.S.A I UK I GERMANY

# GORDON SUTHERLANDs
# DAMN YOU
### BEST TYPING MISTAKES AND AUTOCORRECT FAILS
# FAT FINGERS

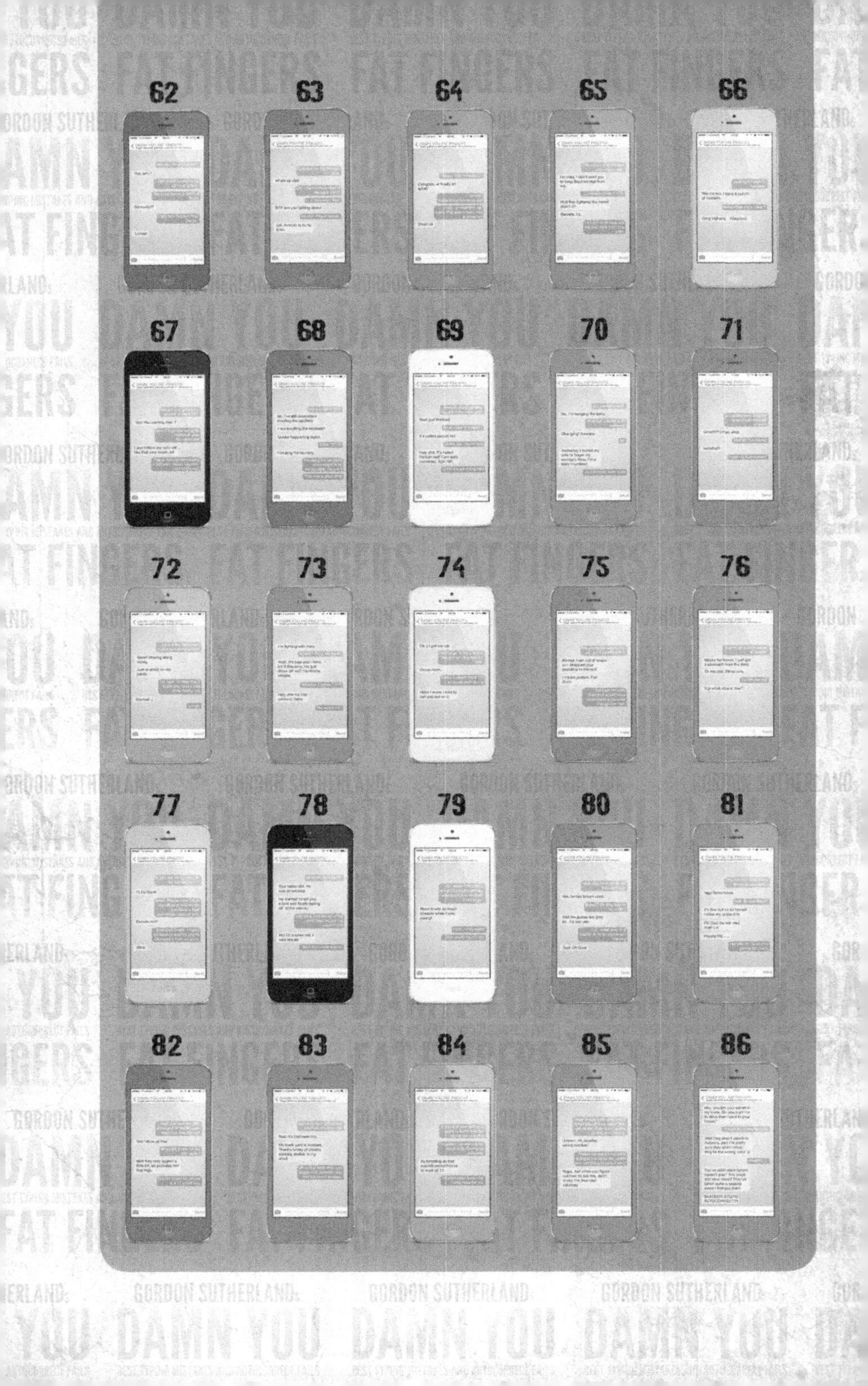

62
63
64
65
66
67
68
69
70
71
72
73
74
75
76
77
78
79
80
81
82
83
84
85
86
GORDON SUTHERLAND
DAMN YOU
FAT FINGERS

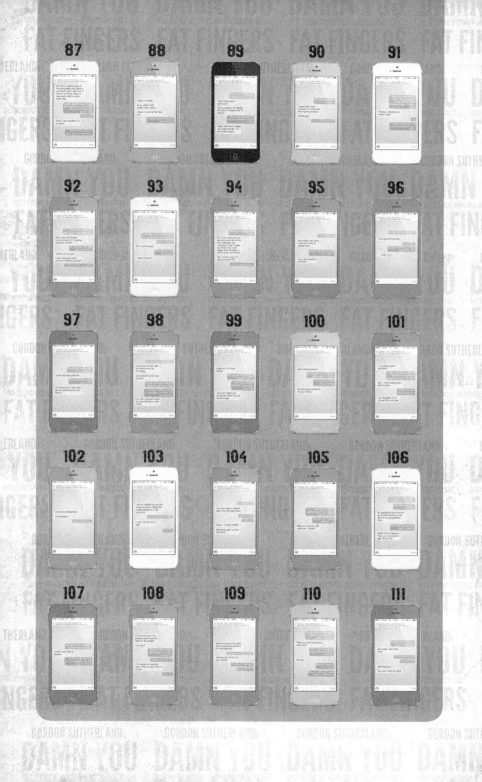

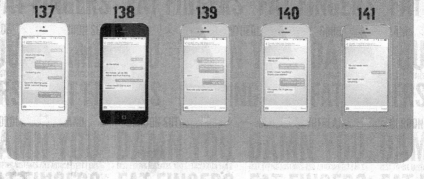

# GORDON SUTHERLANDs
# DAMN YOU
## BEST TYPING MISTAKES AND AUTOCORRECT FAILS
# FAT FINGERS

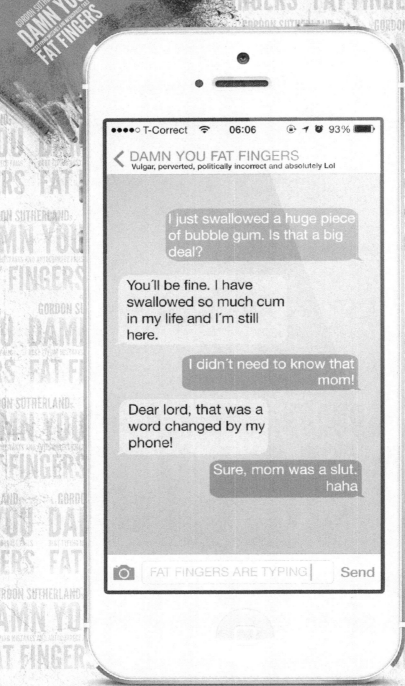

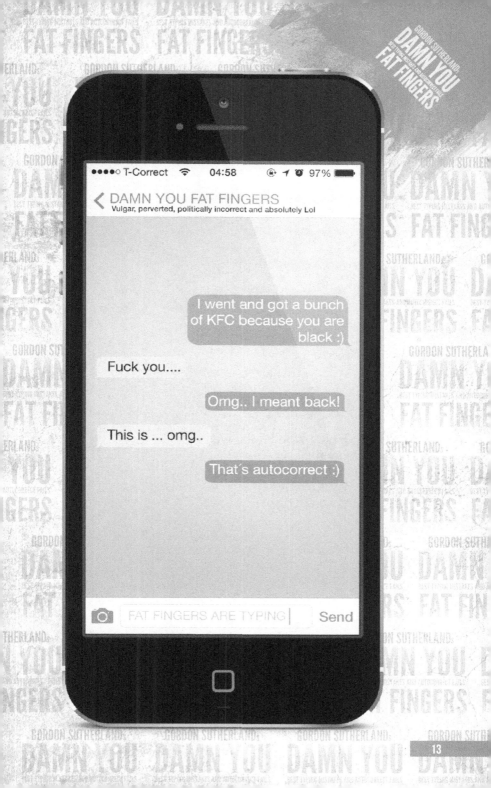

Done all your homework?

Nope I´ve been masturbating. why is it so much fun?

IDK son, I had the same problem too when i was younger.

Huh, I wonder if it was genetics.

Wait...! I meant procrasting.

Well, this is awkward.

FAT FINGERS ARE TYPING |    Send

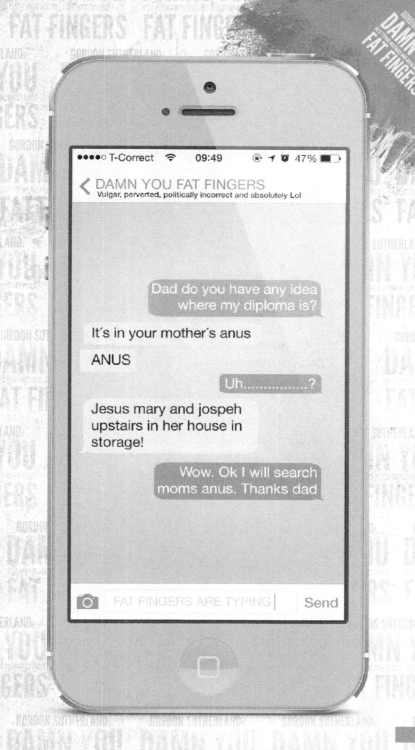

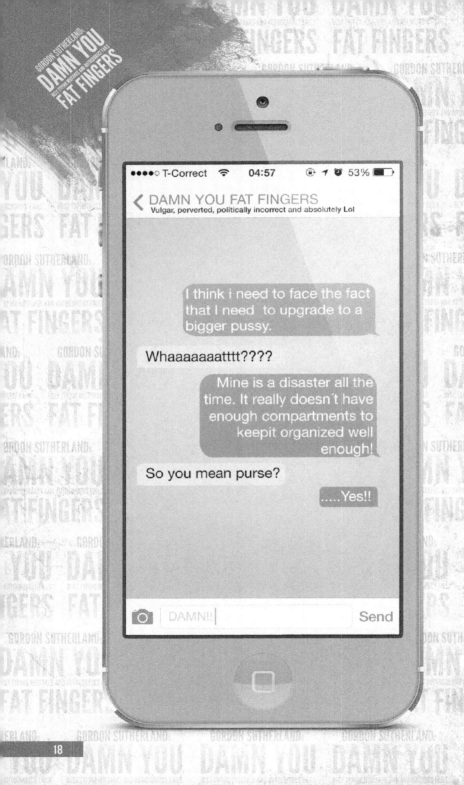

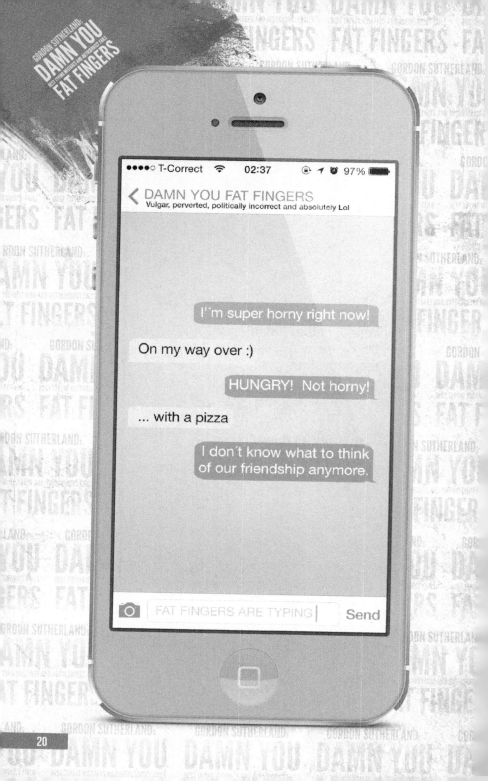

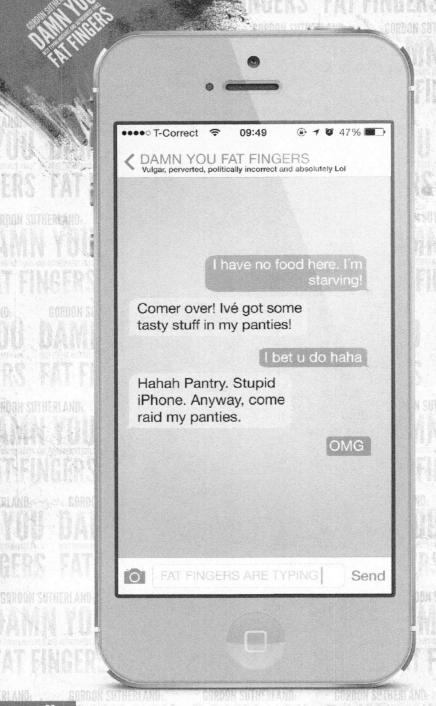

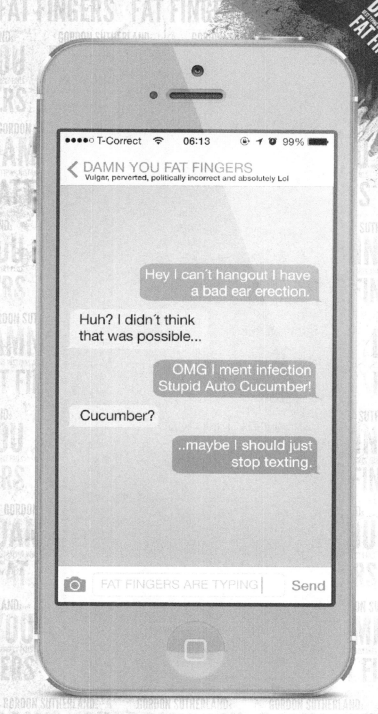

**< DAMN YOU FAT FINGERS**
Vulgar, perverted, politically incorrect and absolutely Lol

> Are you doing the nutcracker this year?

Yep! I'm auctioning kids tomorrow.

Suctioning kids.

Ridiculous auto cat rectal

Birdseed!

I AM AUDITIONING KIDS FORPLAY

> Wow I am sorry I asked! Hahaha

📷 | FAT FINGERS ARE TYPING | | Send

**< DAMN YOU FAT FINGERS**
Vulgar, perverted, politically incorrect and absolutely Lol

Is Dildodorf dead?

Yes mom! Dumbledore is dead.

And snake man is dead also?

Mom! You kidding ?

📷 FAT FINGERS ARE TYPING | Send

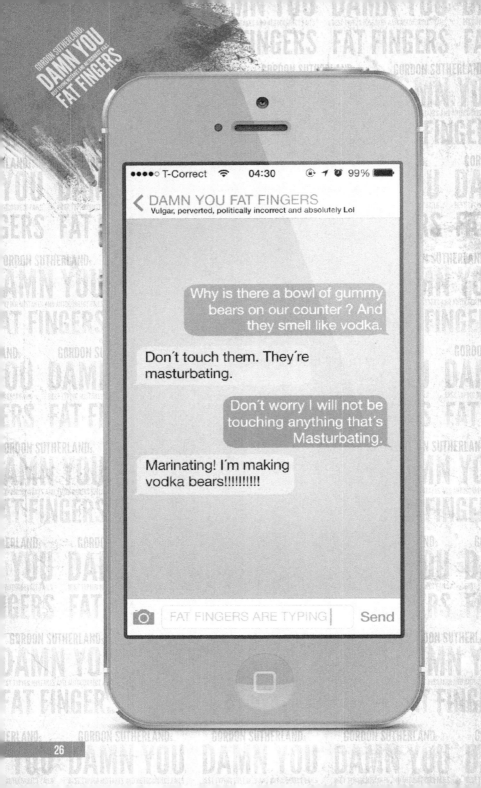

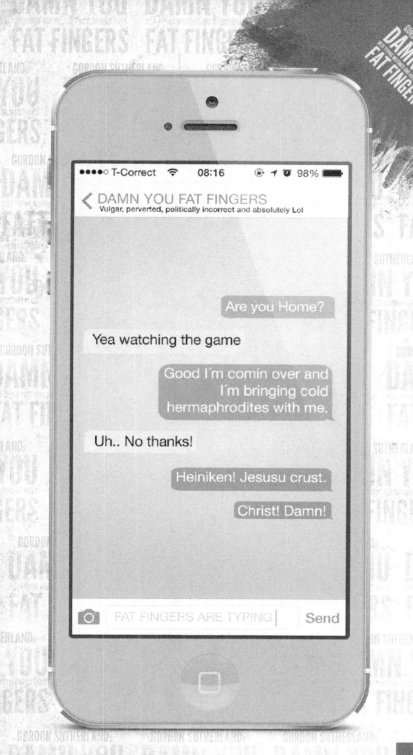

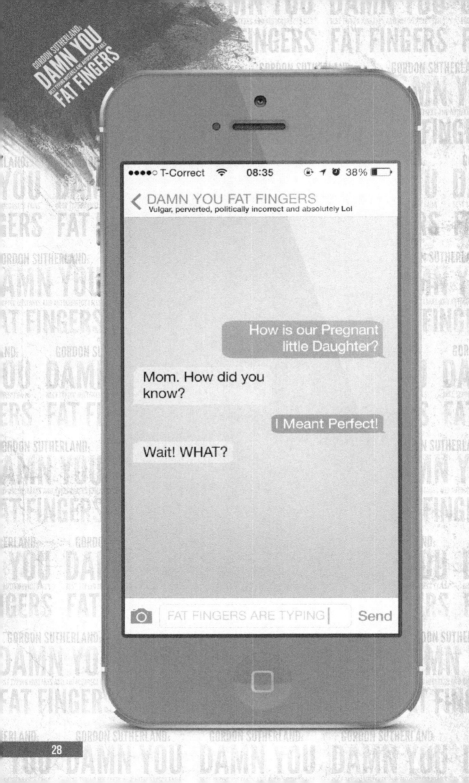

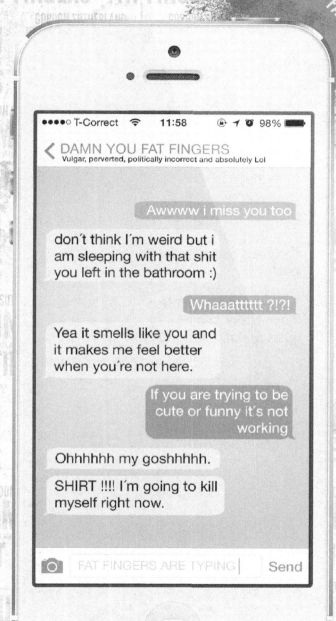

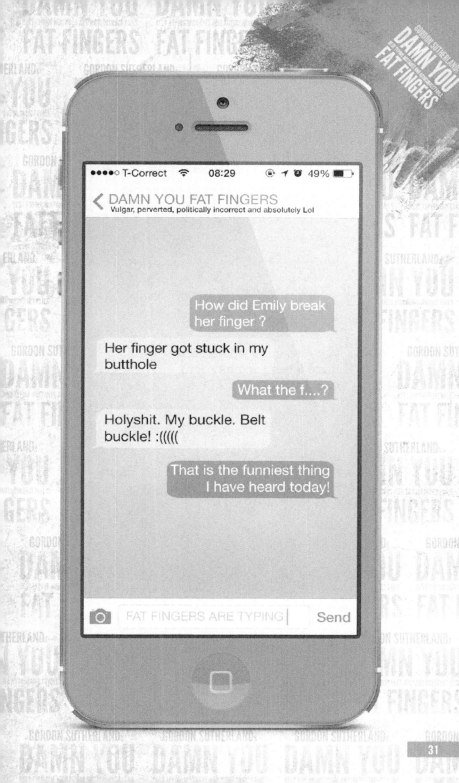

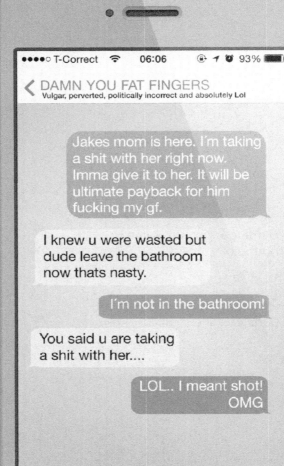

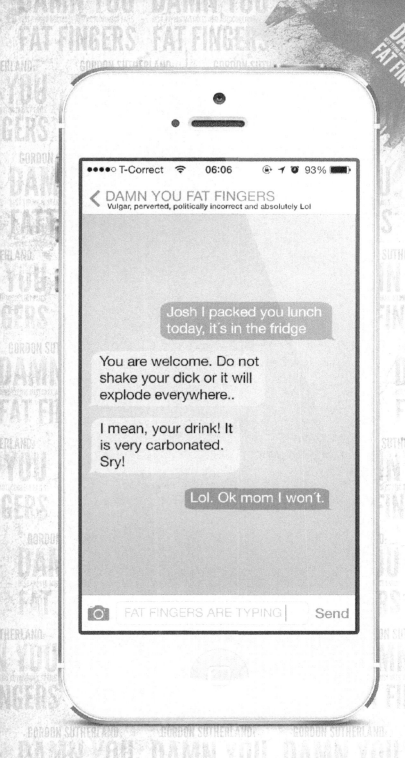

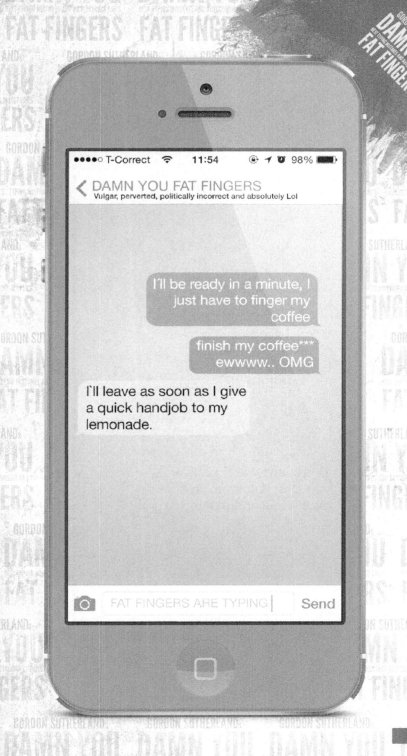

**< DAMN YOU FAT FINGERS**
Vulgar, perverted, politically incorrect and absolutely Lol

> Hey Mr. Barnes. I'm really upset with my last test grade. Can is sex it up with you after school?

Come later after school so no teachers see us. B+ all right? I'm getting horny just thinking about you.

> Umm. Mr Barnes. I meant to say make it up with you.

This is awkward! I'll give you an A if you never repeat this and delete.

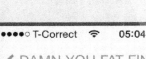

📷  FAT FINGERS ARE TYPING |   Send

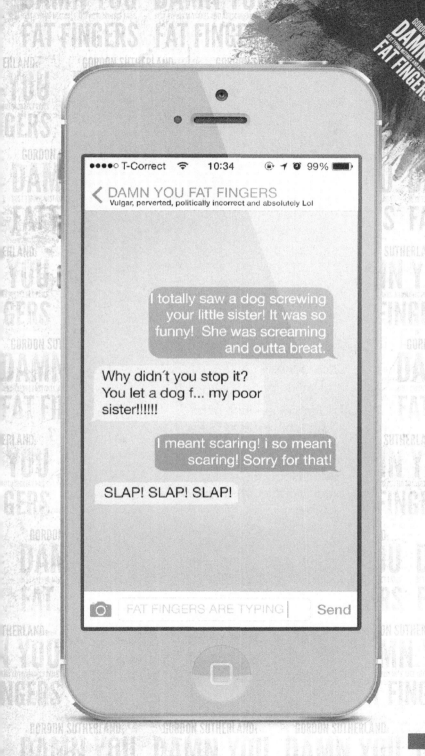

Did u take my call of duty disk for the PS3?

Yes I was wondering when you where gonna figure that out.

Not cool! Driving over there to tickle your ass

ohhh ...dude ... wtf is that?

God Damn It! KICK! Im gonna kick your ass

You are not getting anywhere near my ass :P

FAT FINGERS ARE TYPING | Send

39

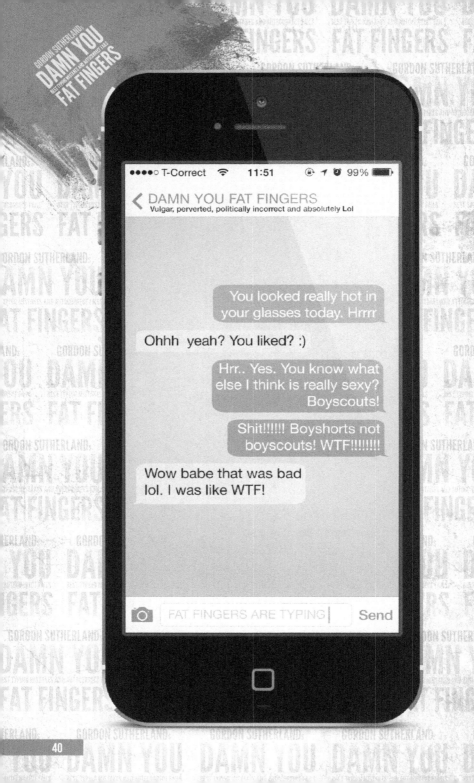

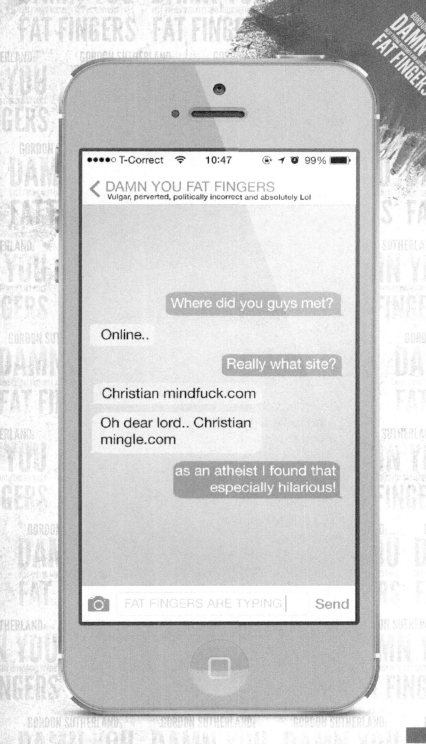

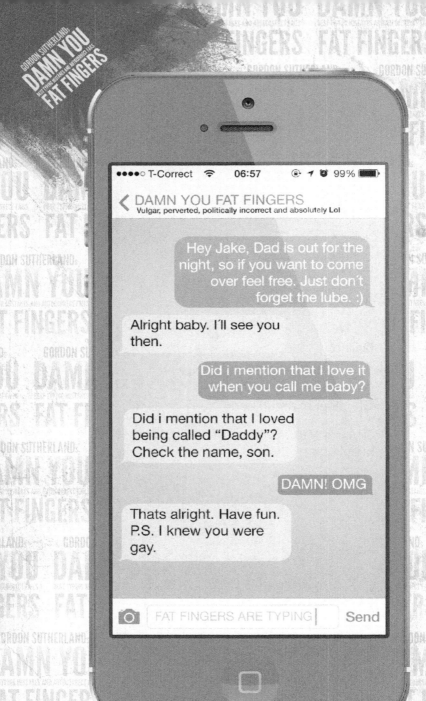

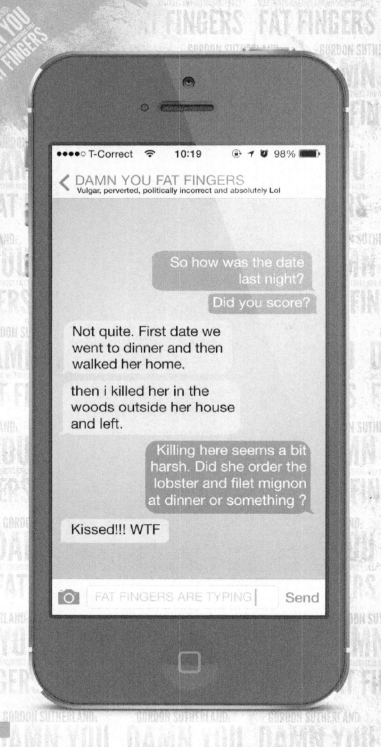

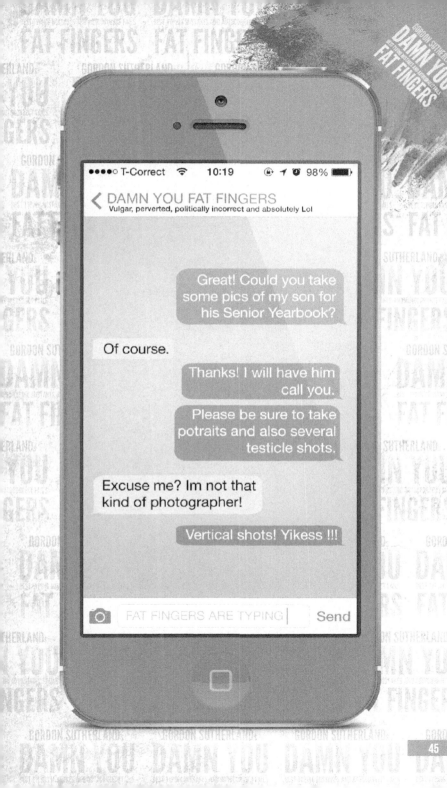

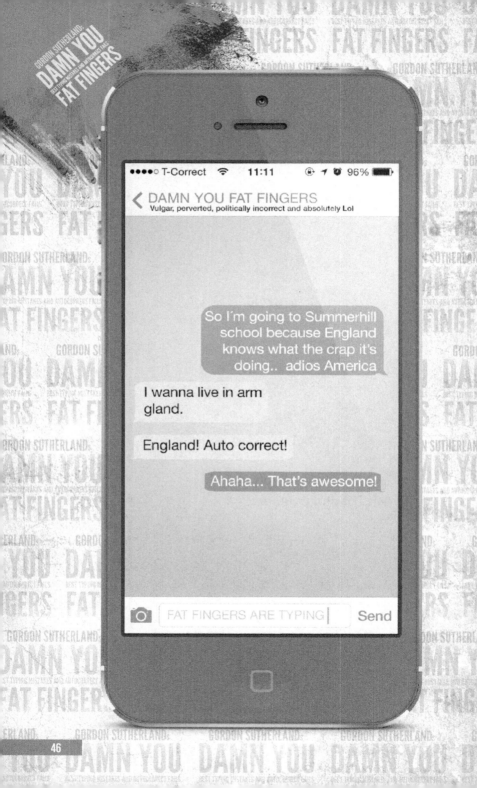

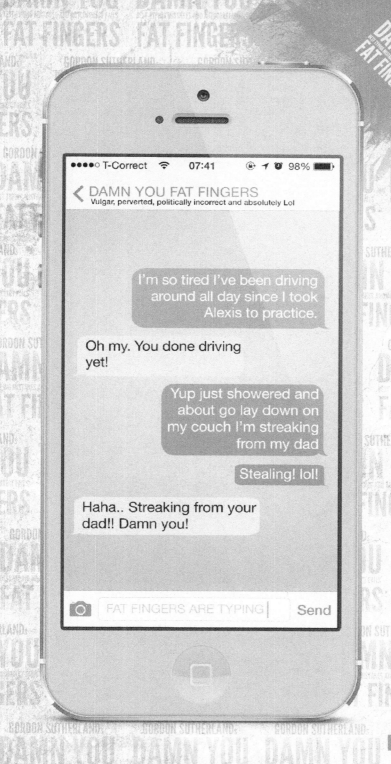

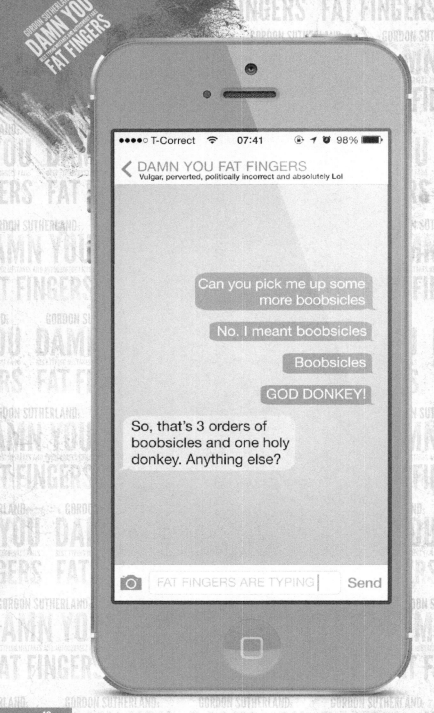

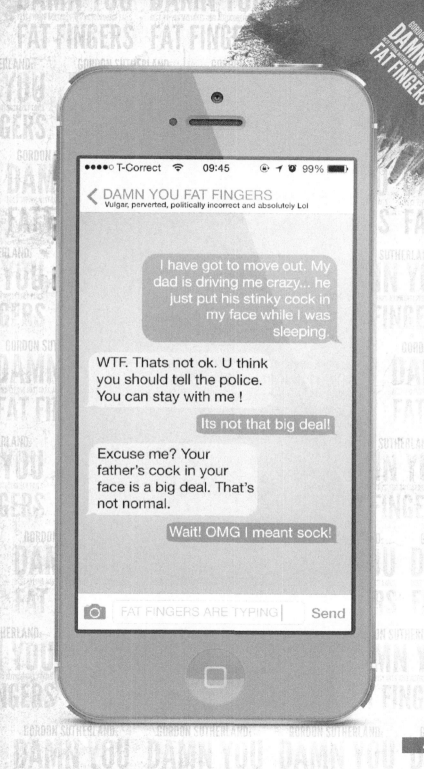

●●●●○ T-Correct 📶 11:05 ⚙ ✈ 🔋 99% 🔋

**‹ DAMN YOU FAT FINGERS**
Vulgar, perverted, politically incorrect and absolutely Lol

I'm at karens house

I don't know if I can believe you

You lie to me all the time. You know its not good to lie to your father.

It is the truth. I swallow!

SWEAR! I typed swear.

COME HOME NOW.

📷 | FAT FINGERS ARE TYPING | | Send

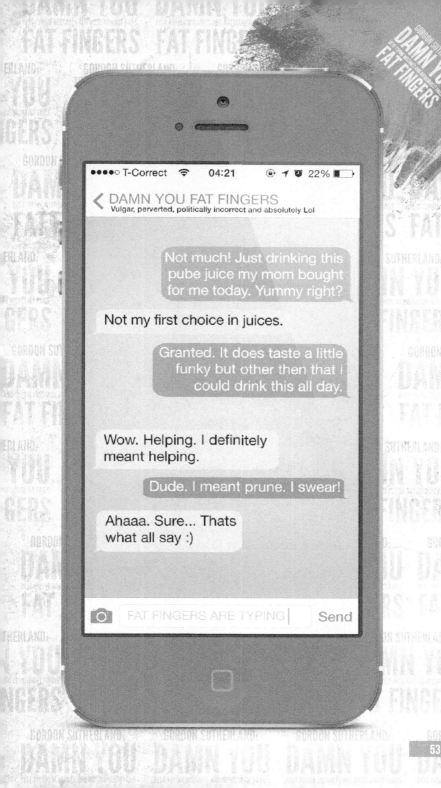

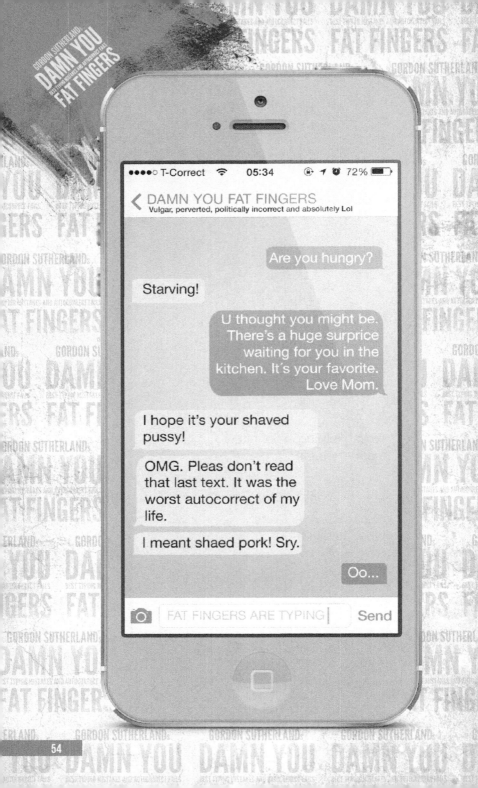

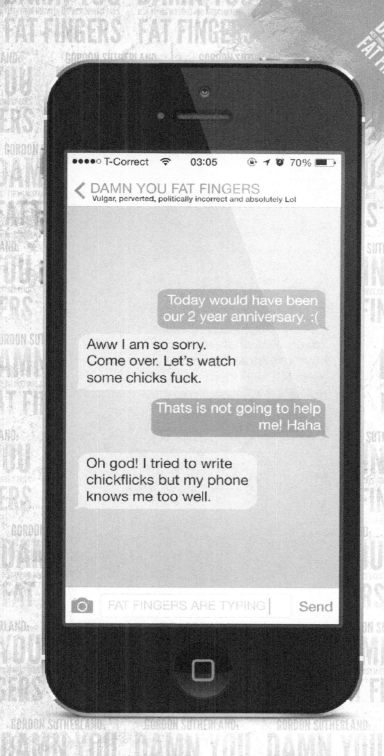

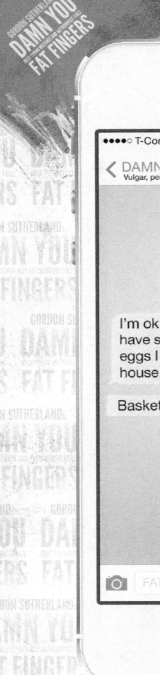

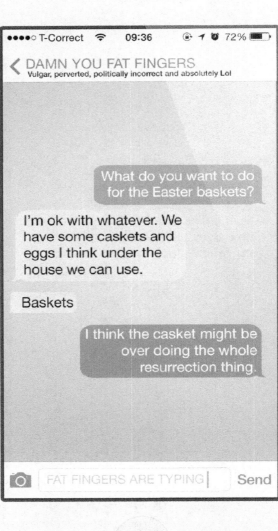

What do you want to do for the Easter baskets?

I'm ok with whatever. We have some caskets and eggs I think under the house we can use.

Baskets

I think the casket might be over doing the whole resurrection thing.

📷 FAT FINGERS ARE TYPING |    Send

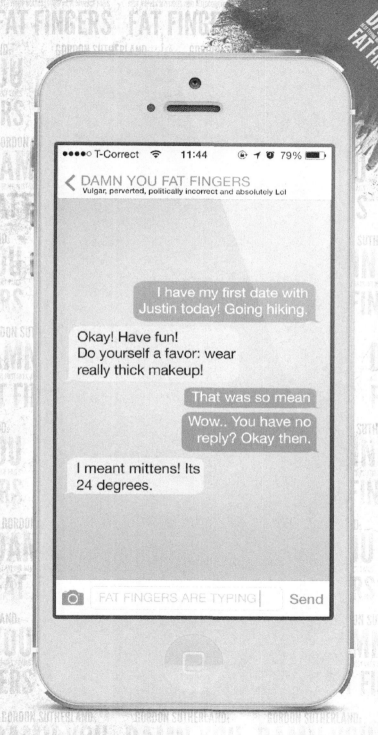

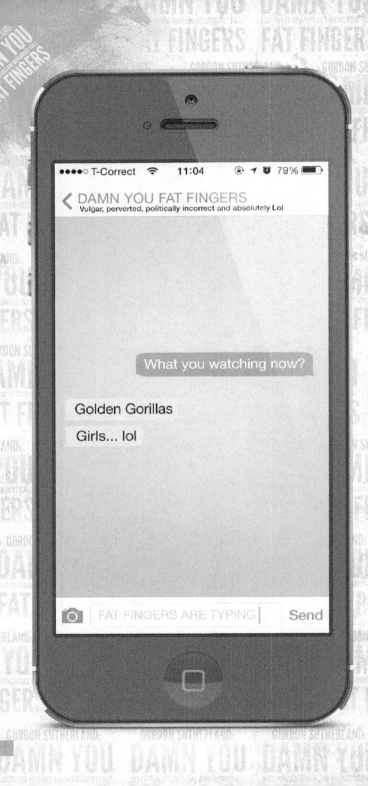

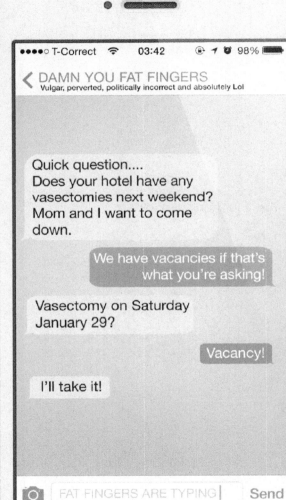

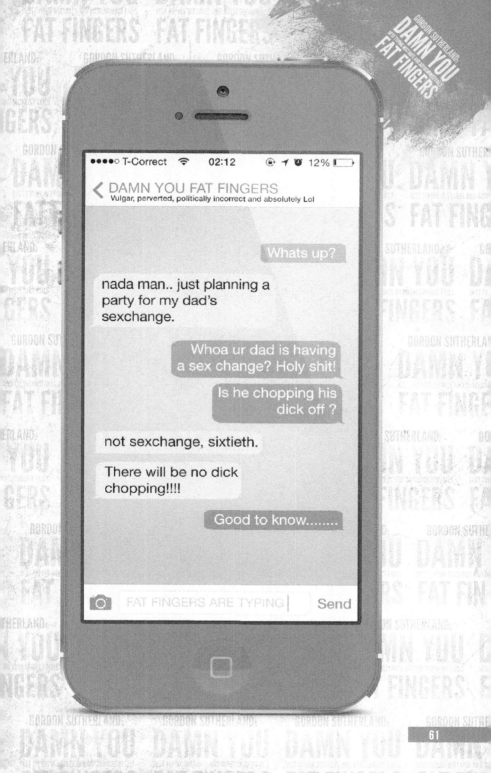

●●●●○ T-Correct 🗢 02:12 📍 ✈ ⏰ 12% 🔋

**< DAMN YOU FAT FINGERS**
Vulgar, perverted, politically incorrect and absolutely Lol

Whats up?

nada man.. just planning a party for my dad's sexchange.

Whoa ur dad is having a sex change? Holy shit!

Is he chopping his dick off ?

not sexchange, sixtieth.

There will be no dick chopping!!!!

Good to know........

📷 FAT FINGERS ARE TYPING|    Send

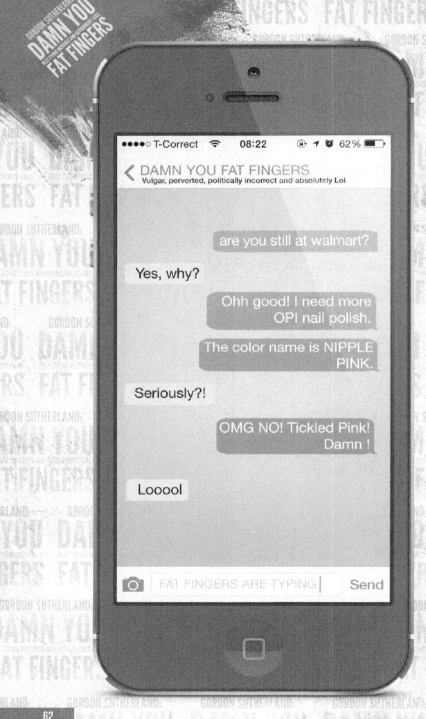

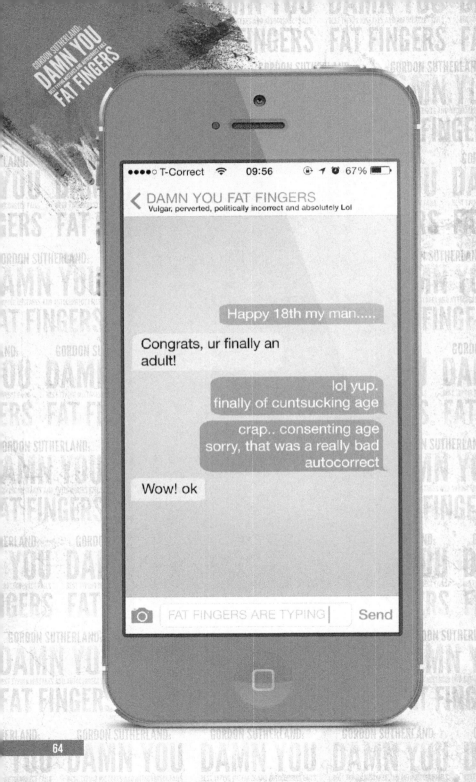

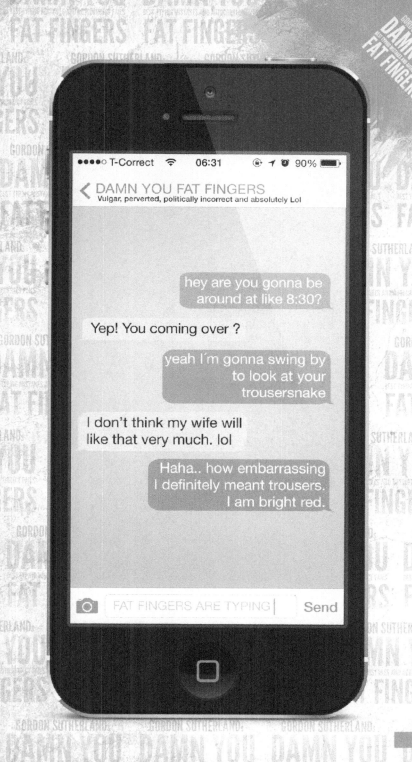

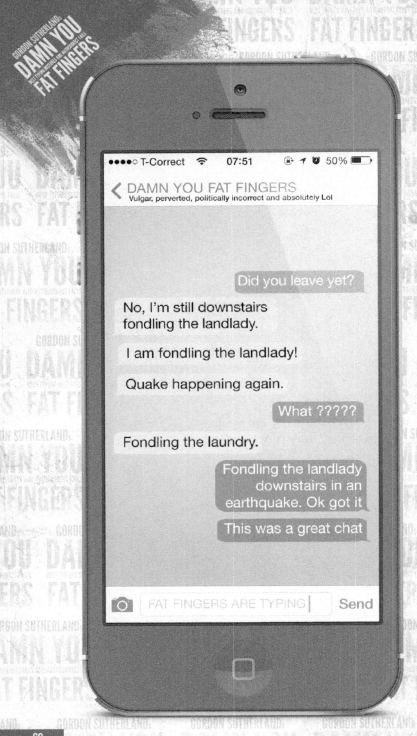

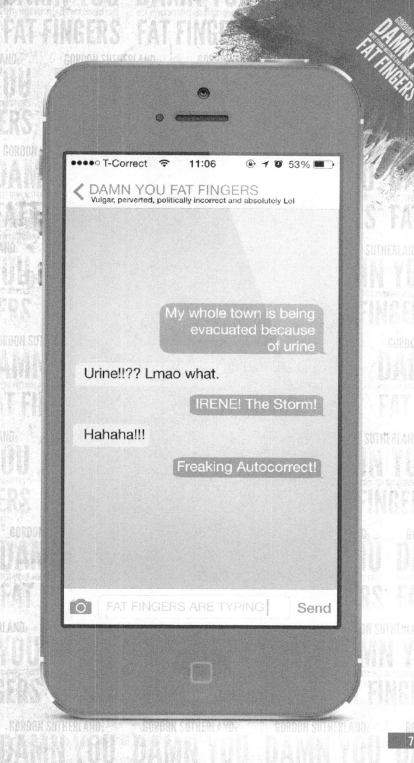

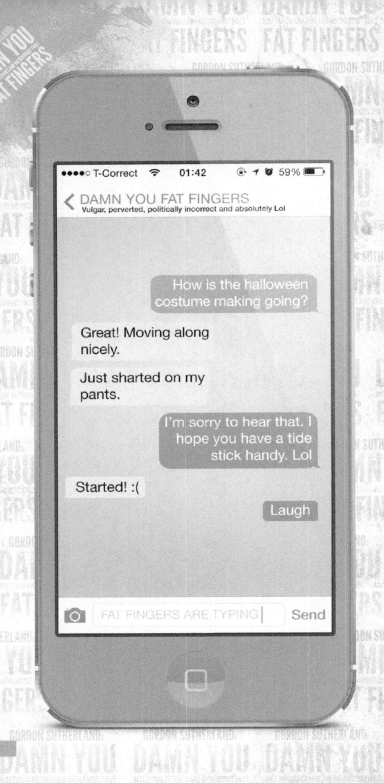

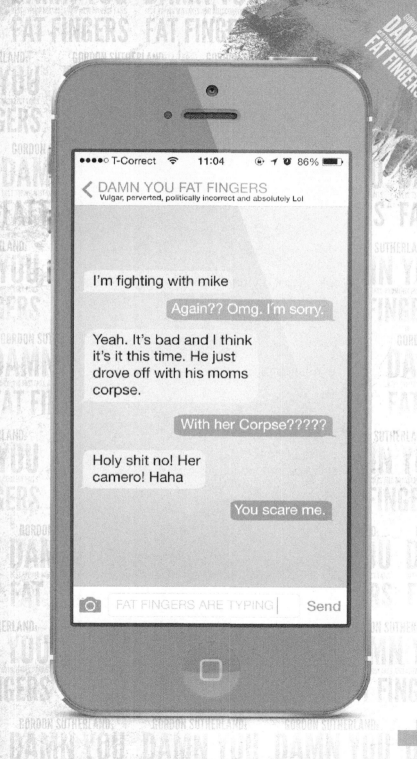

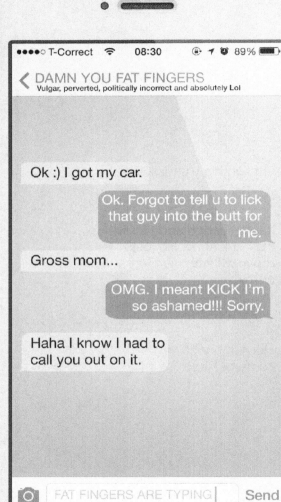

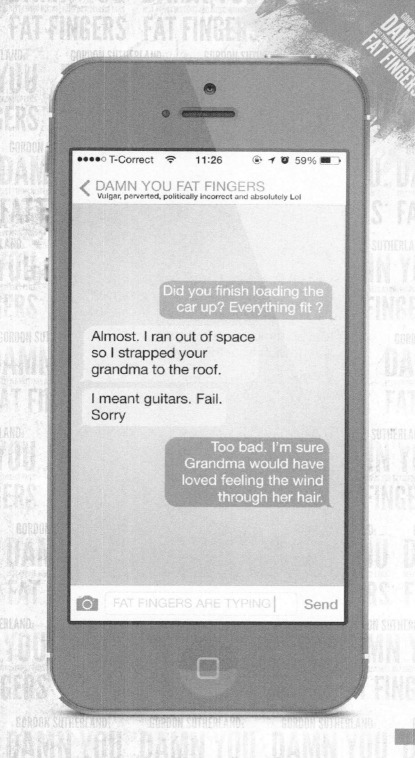

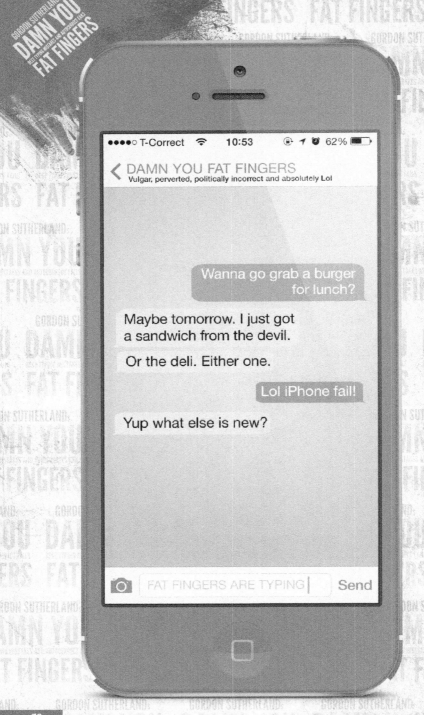

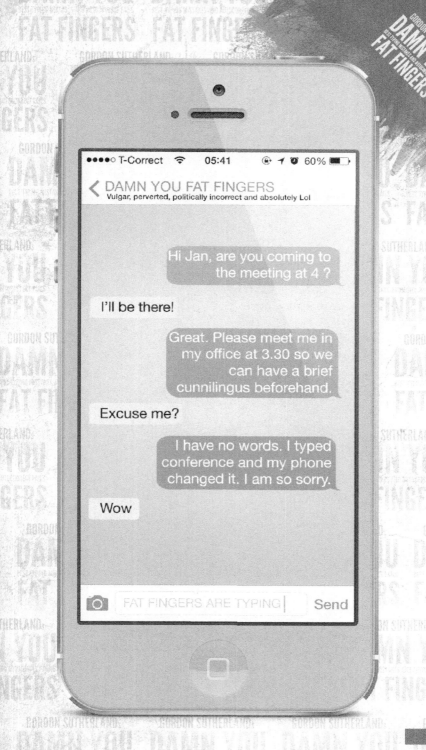

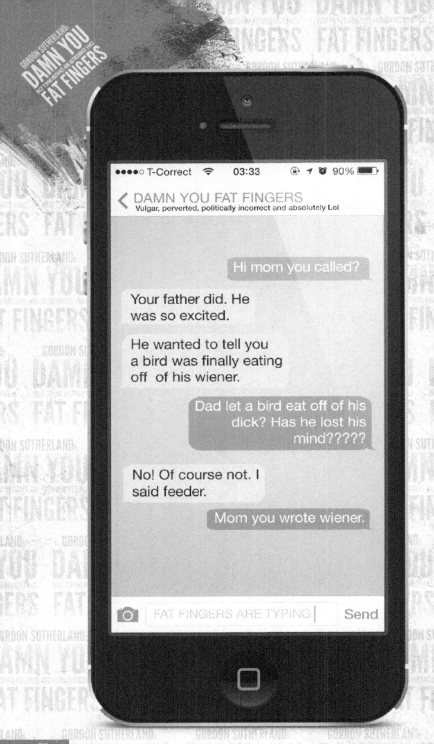

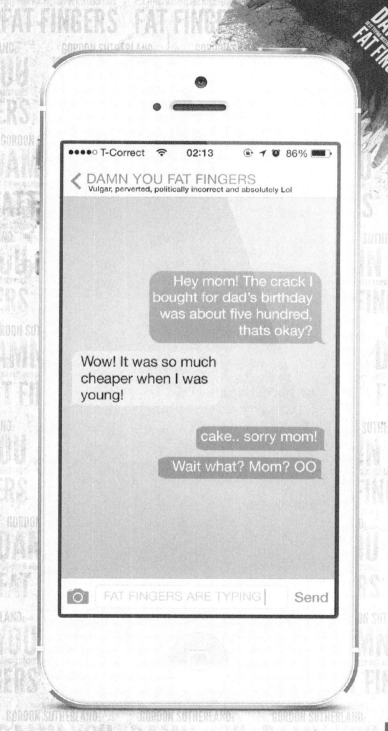

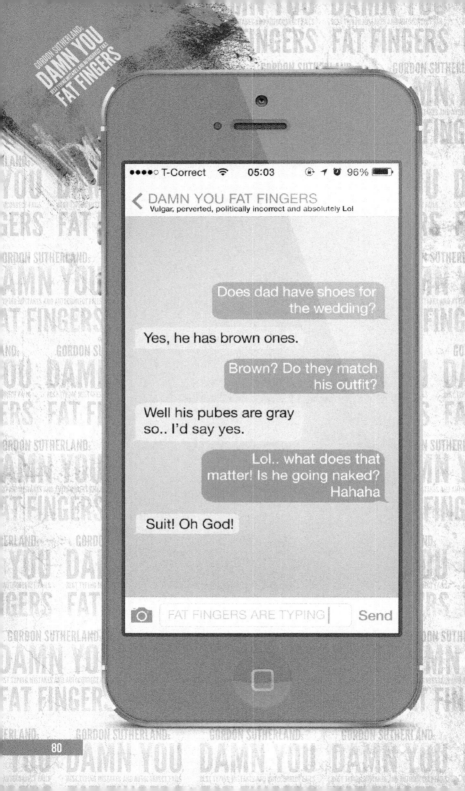

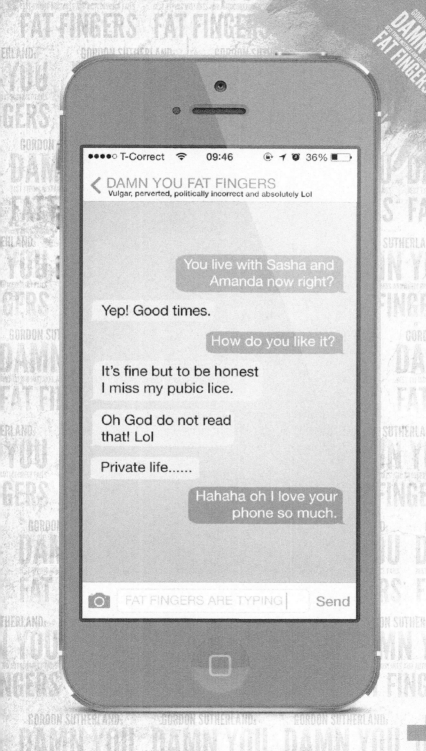

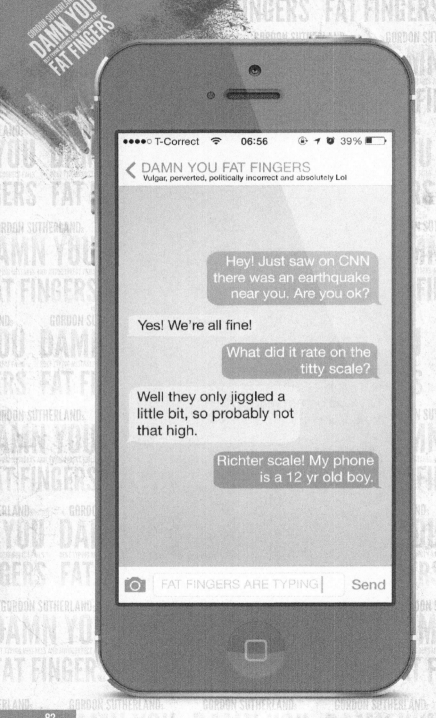

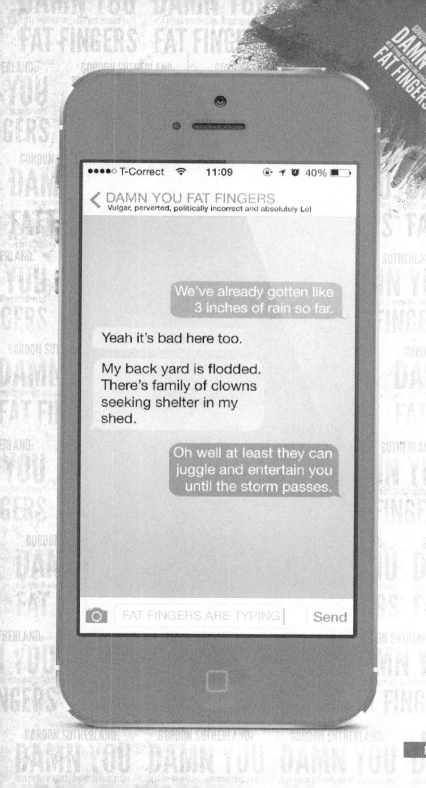

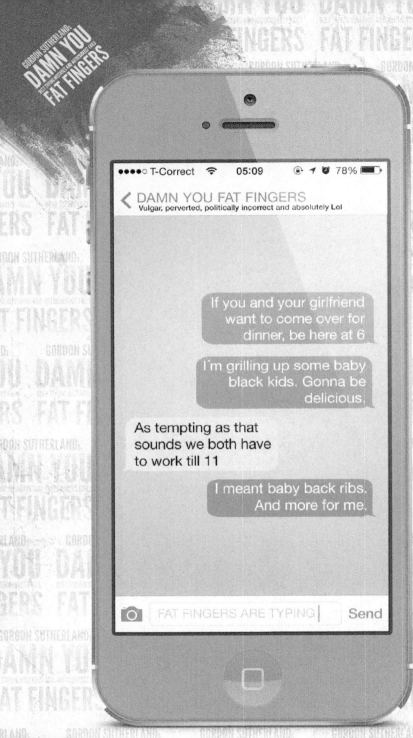

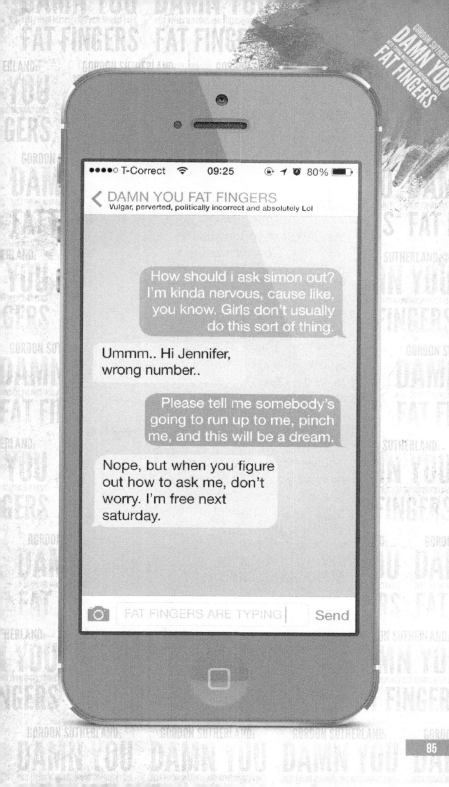

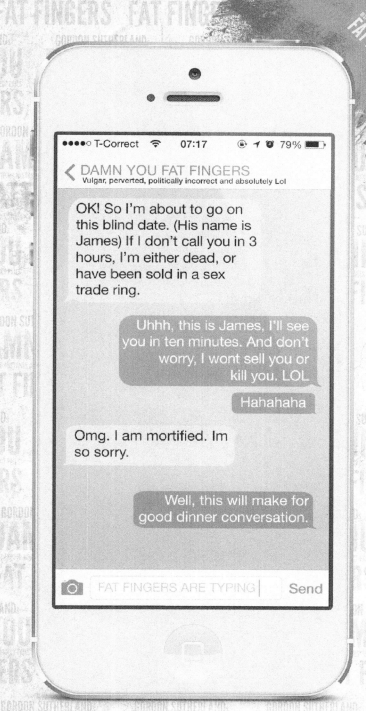

OK! So I'm about to go on this blind date. (His name is James) If I don't call you in 3 hours, I'm either dead, or have been sold in a sex trade ring.

Uhhh, this is James, I'll see you in ten minutes. And don't worry, I wont sell you or kill you. LOL

Hahahaha

Omg. I am mortified. Im so sorry.

Well, this will make for good dinner conversation.

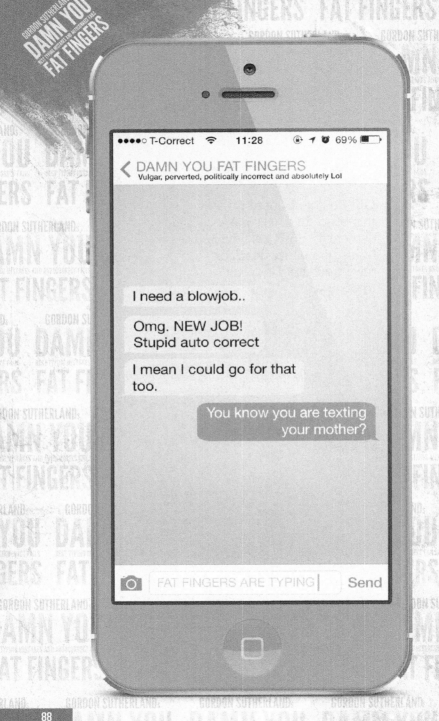

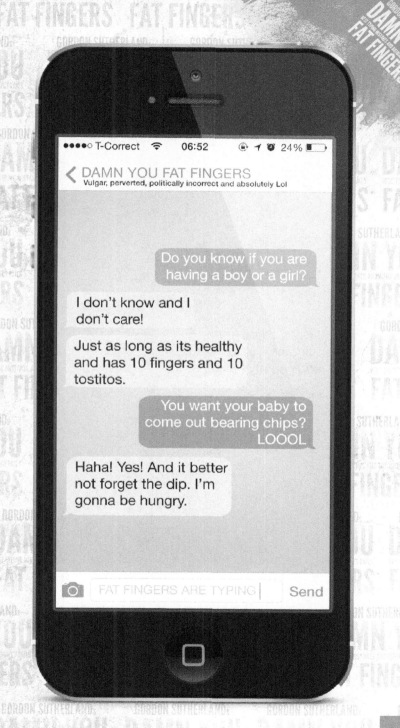

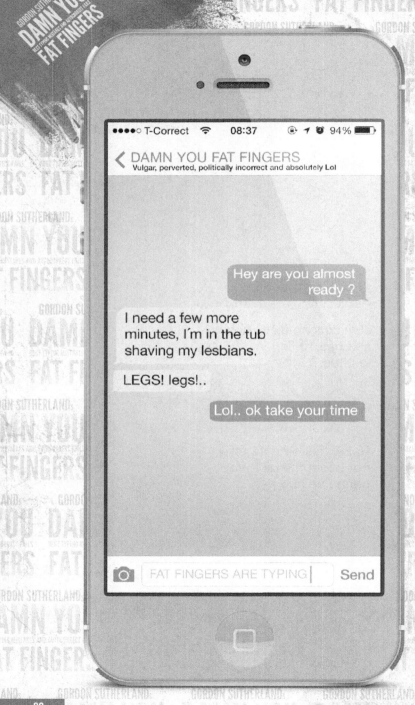

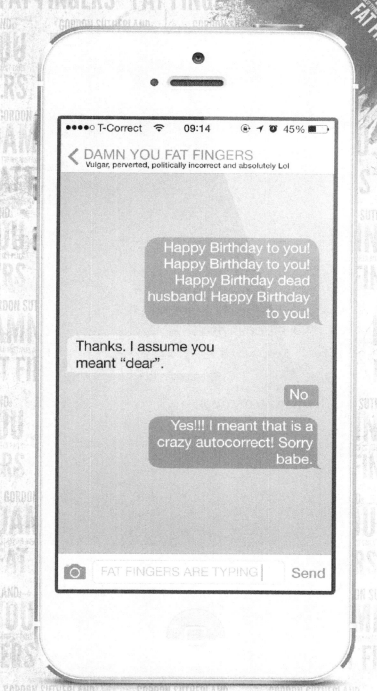

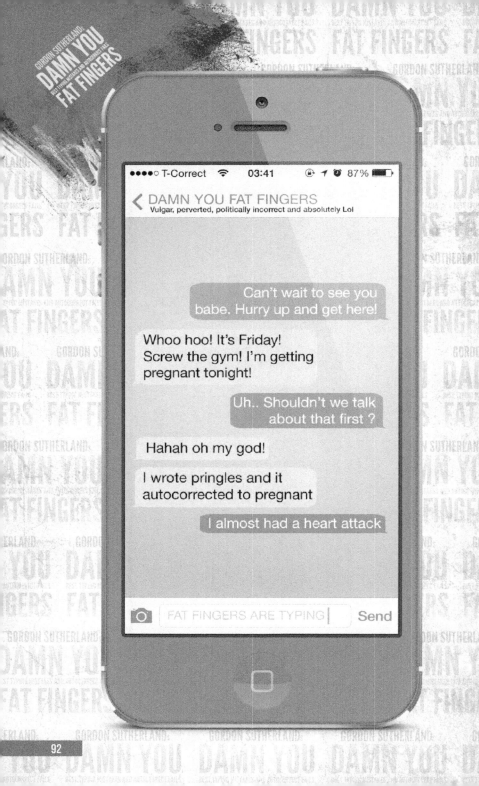

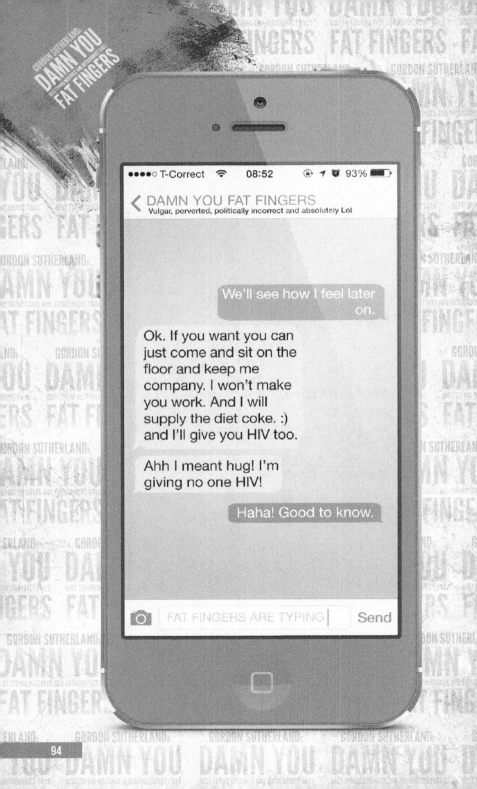

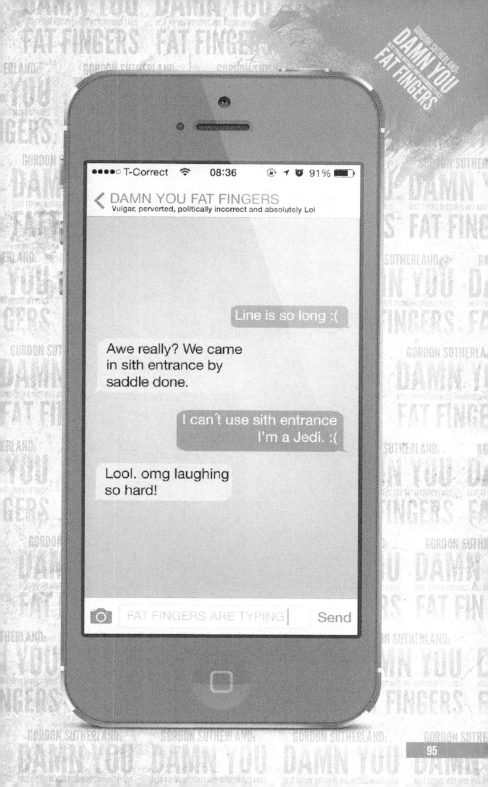

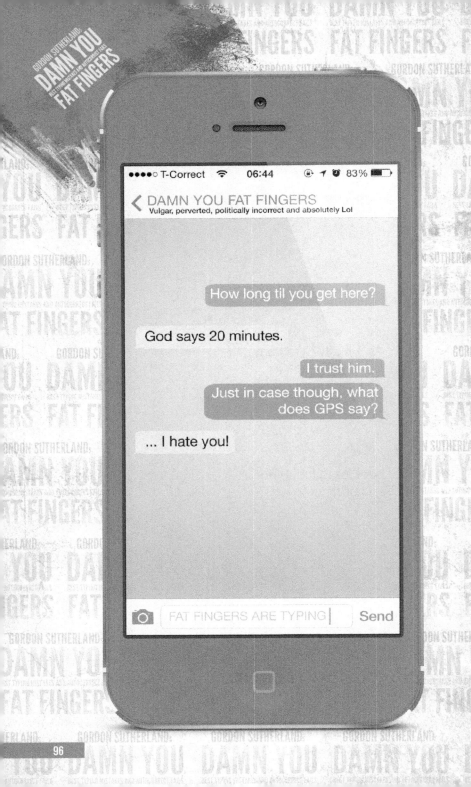

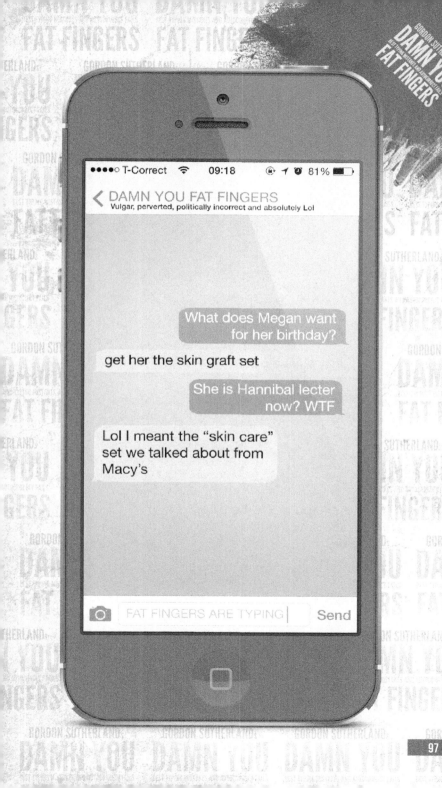

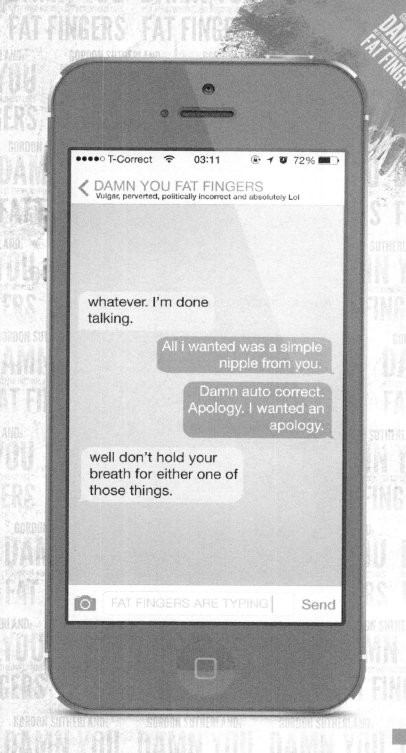

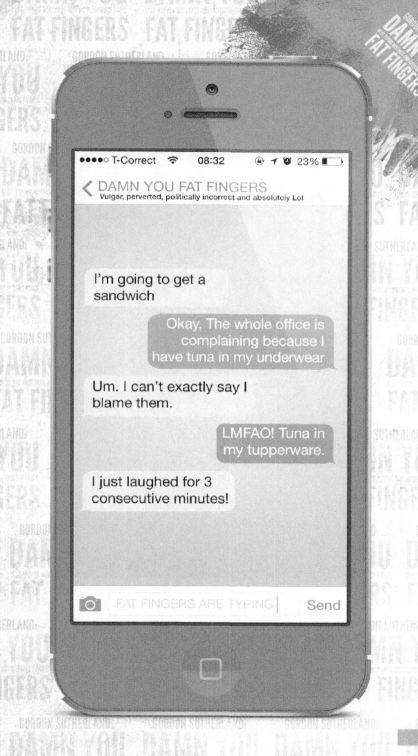

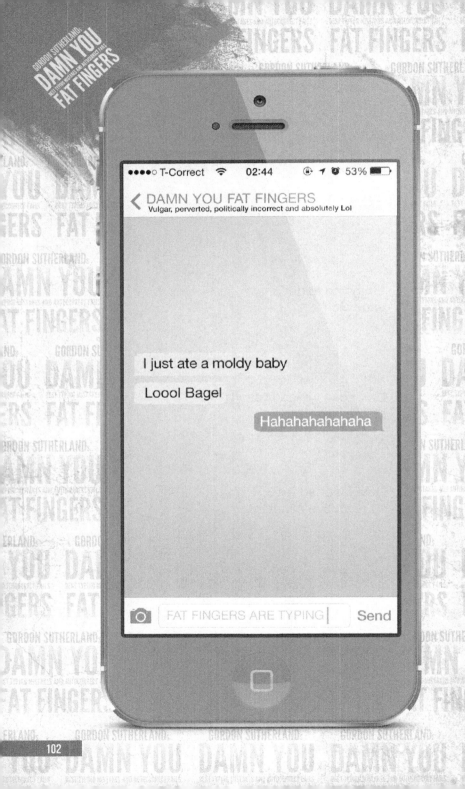

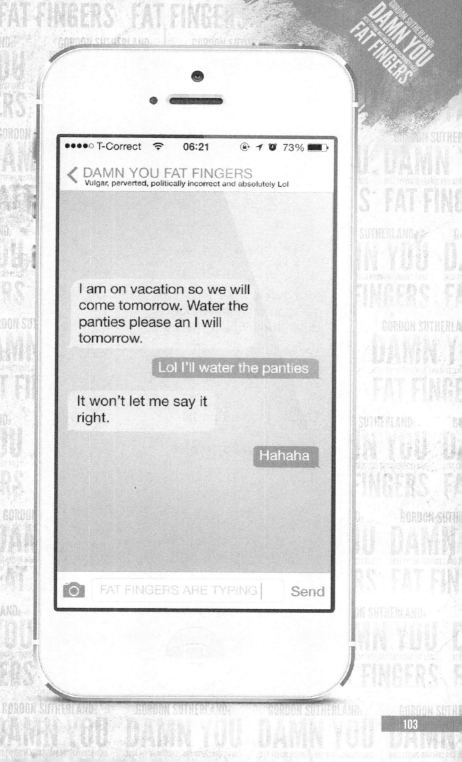

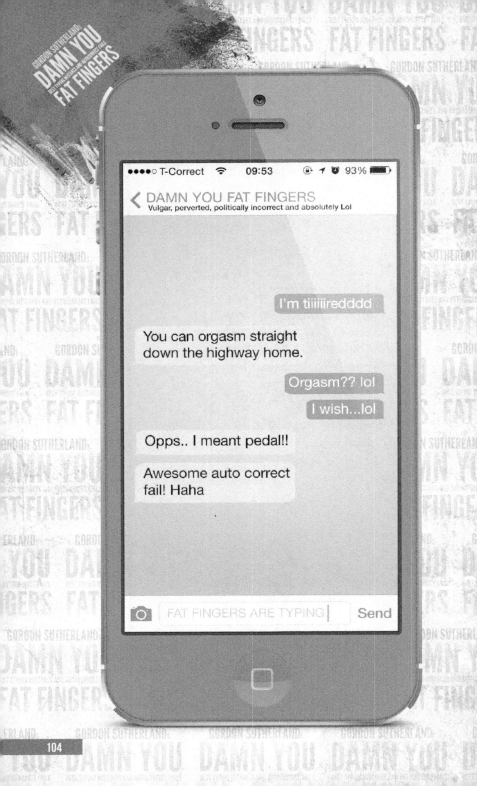

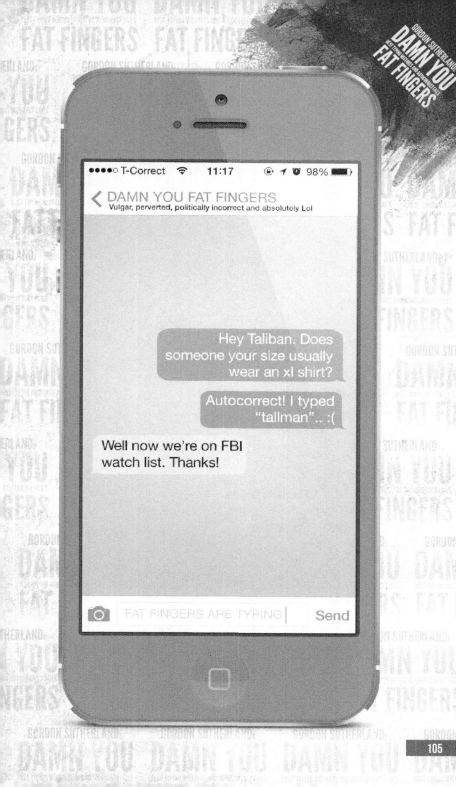

## ‹ DAMN YOU FAT FINGERS
Vulgar, perverted, politically incorrect and absolutely Lol

> I'm heading to your place be there in 15 minutes.

> Can we eat first, I'm starving.

An applebee's just opened down the street from me. We can go get diarrhea there.

> Haha that is propbably really accurate.

LMAO that is hilarious. Yeah, you're probably right. Pizza it is.

📷 | FAT FINGERS ARE TYPING | | Send

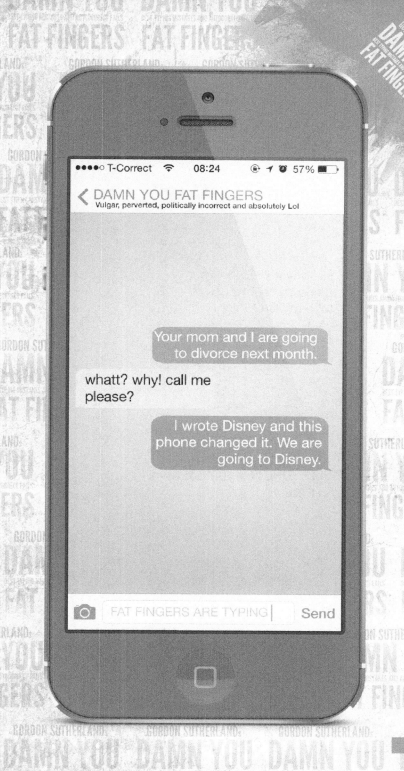

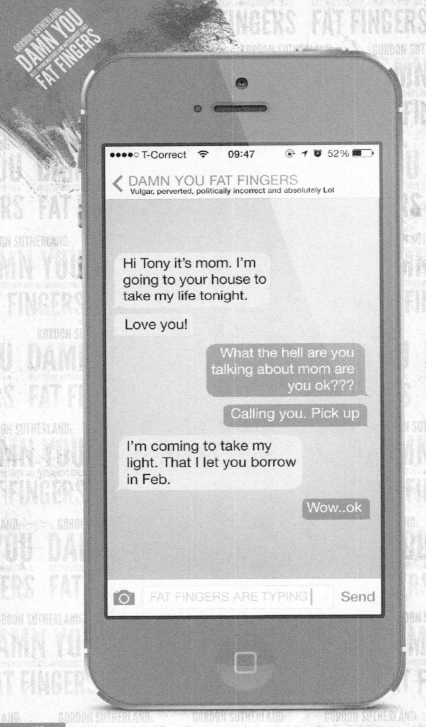

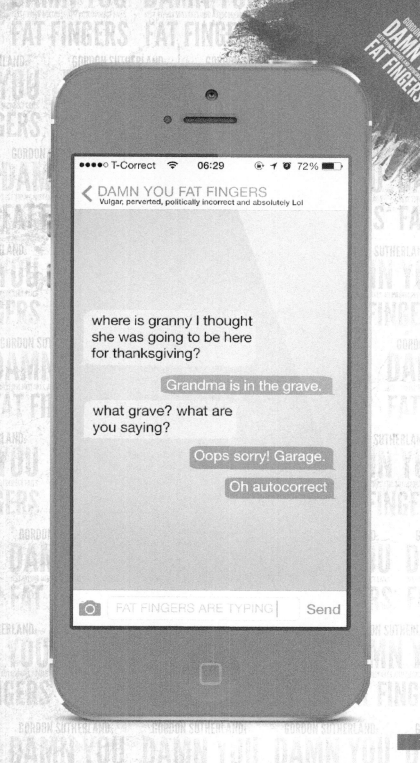

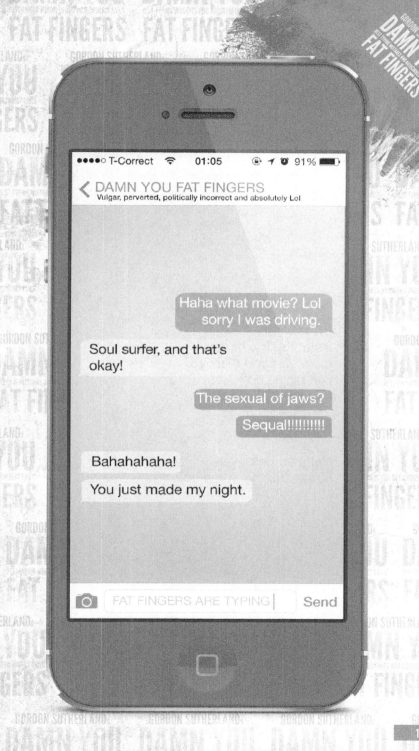

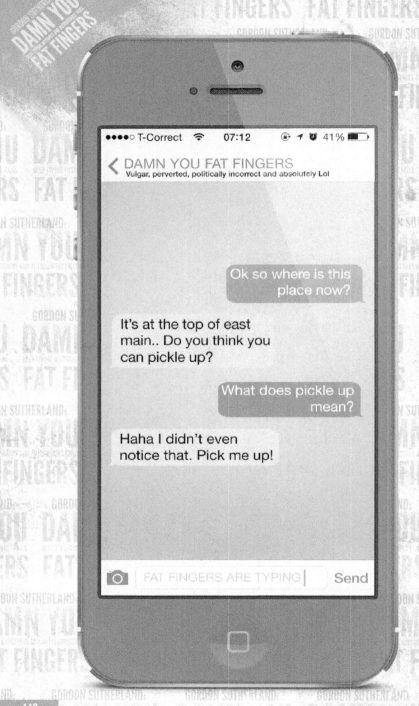

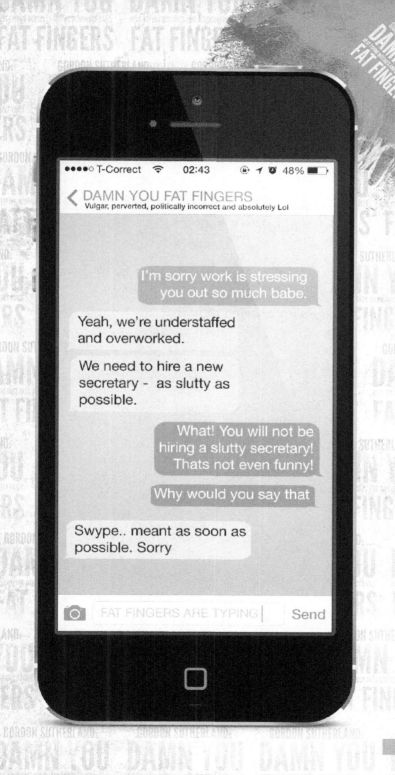

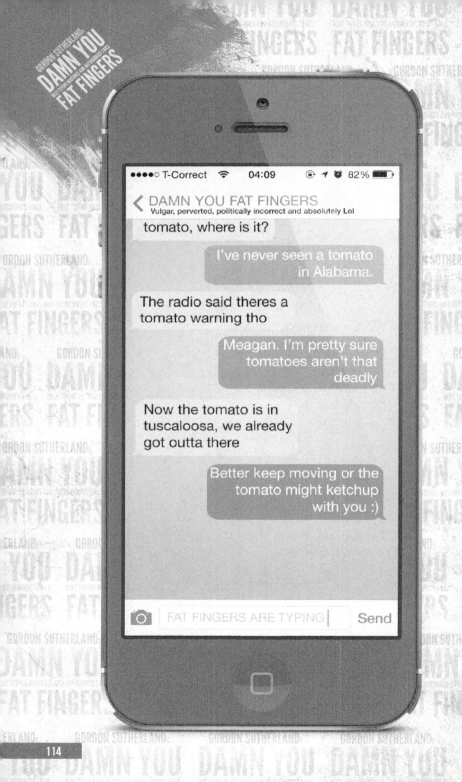

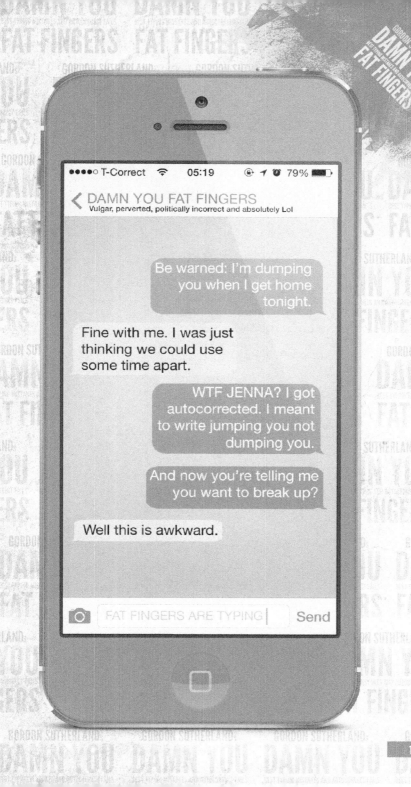

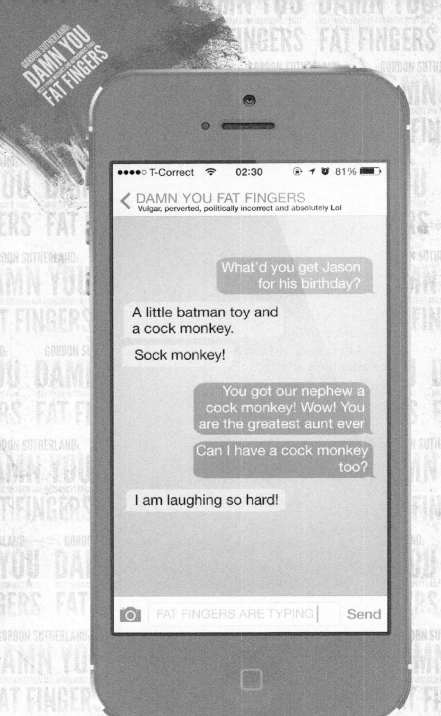

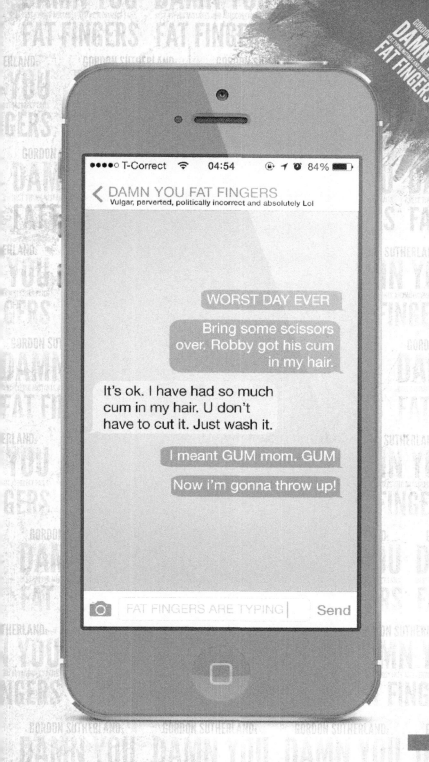

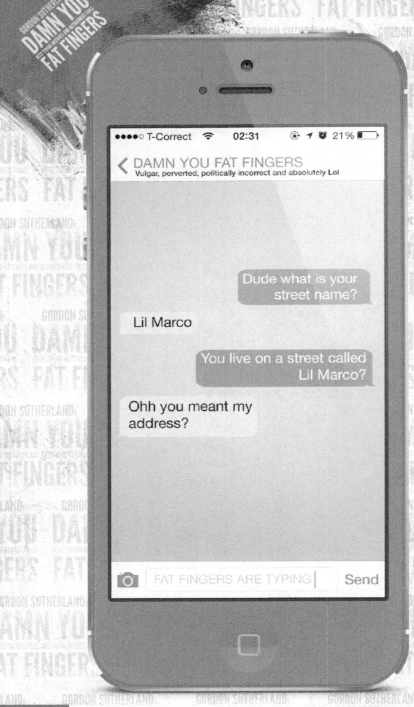

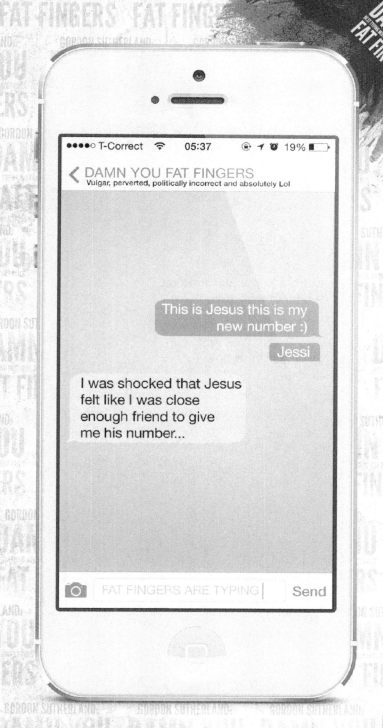

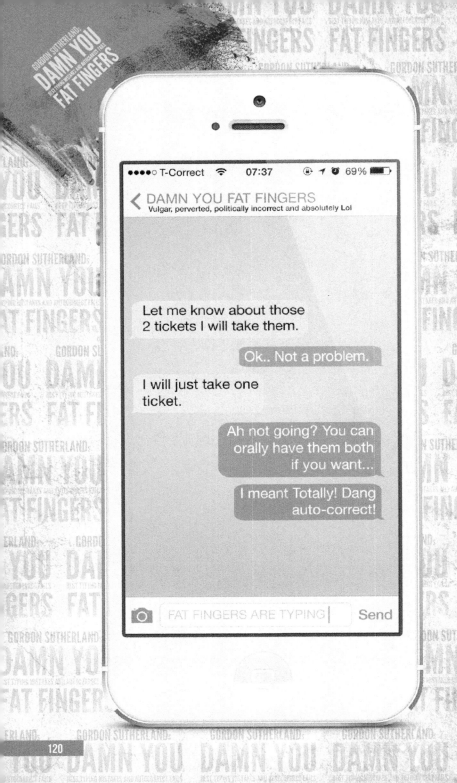

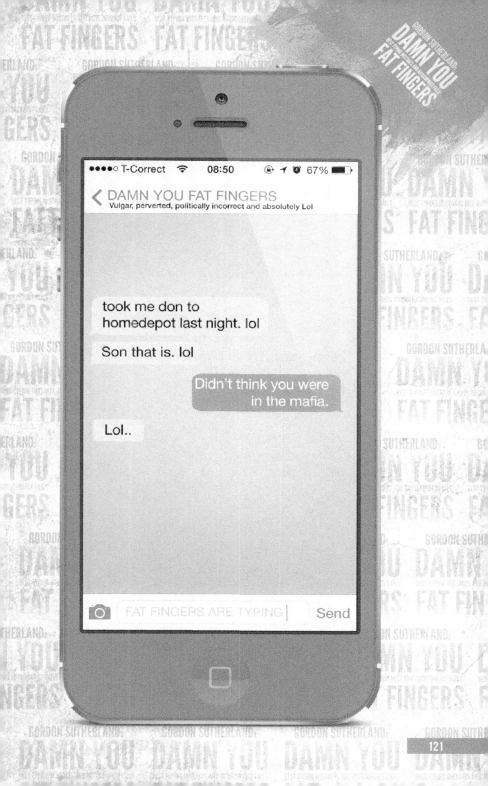

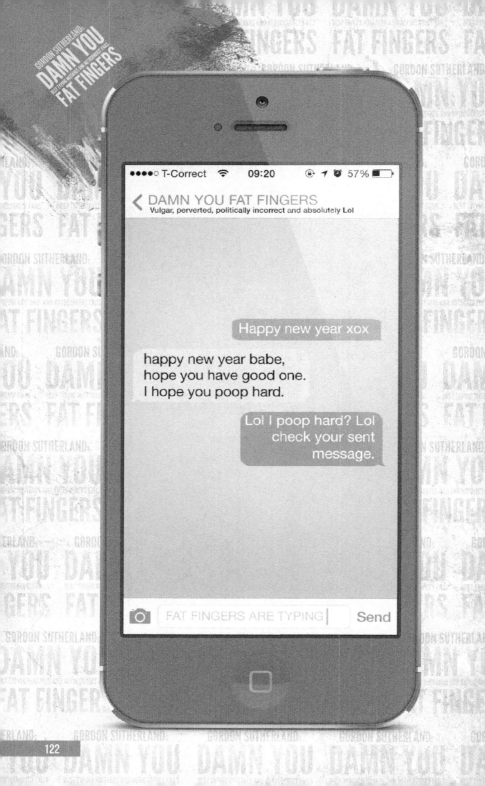

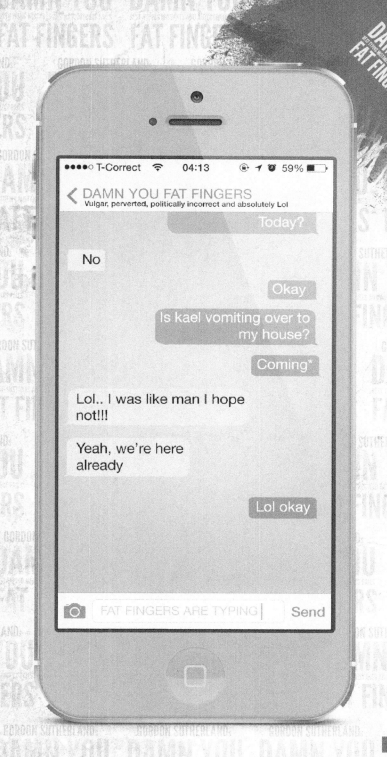

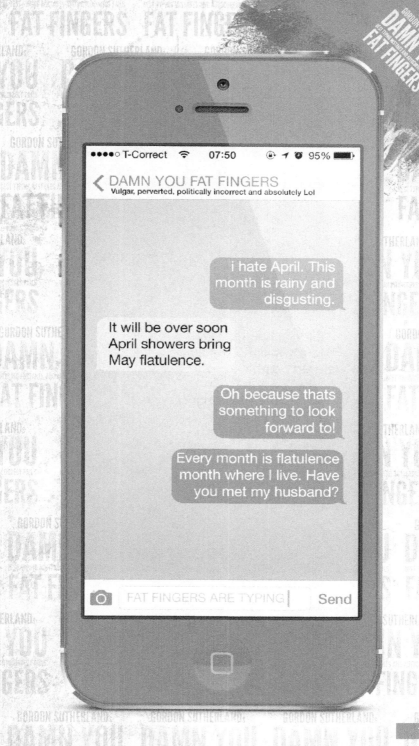

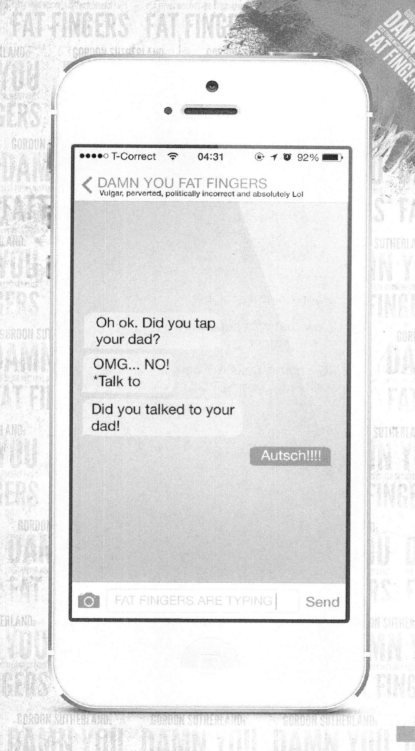

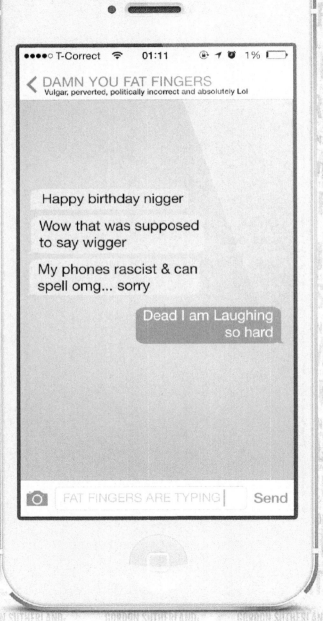

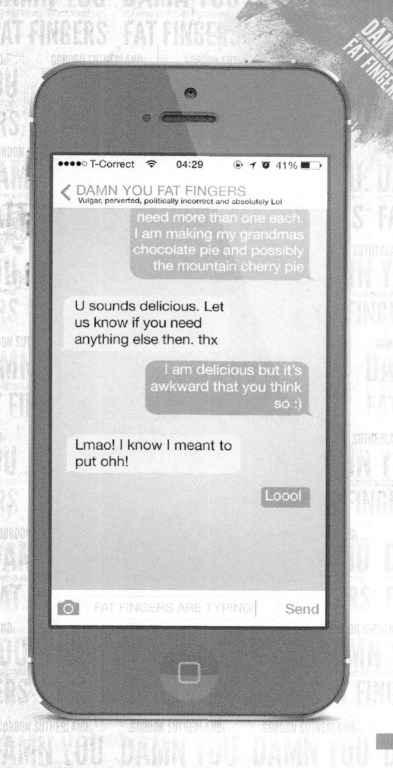

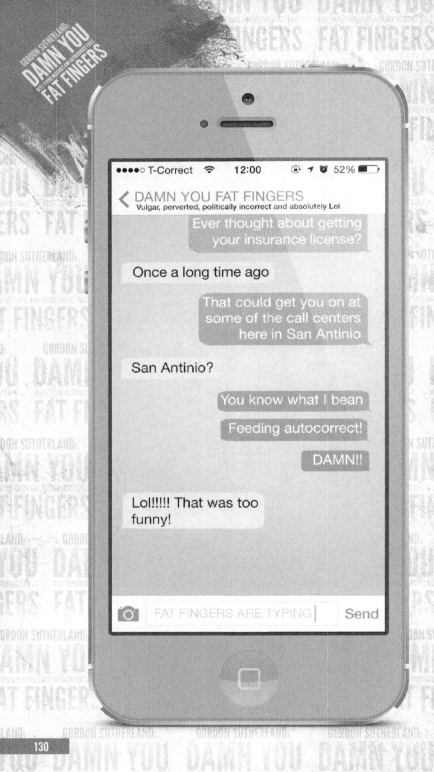

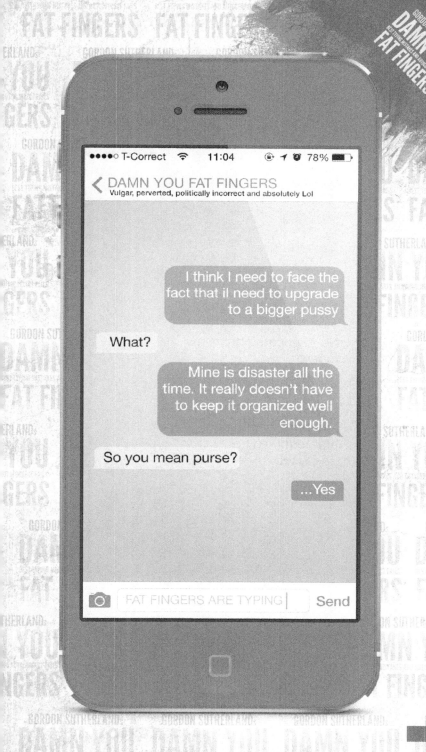

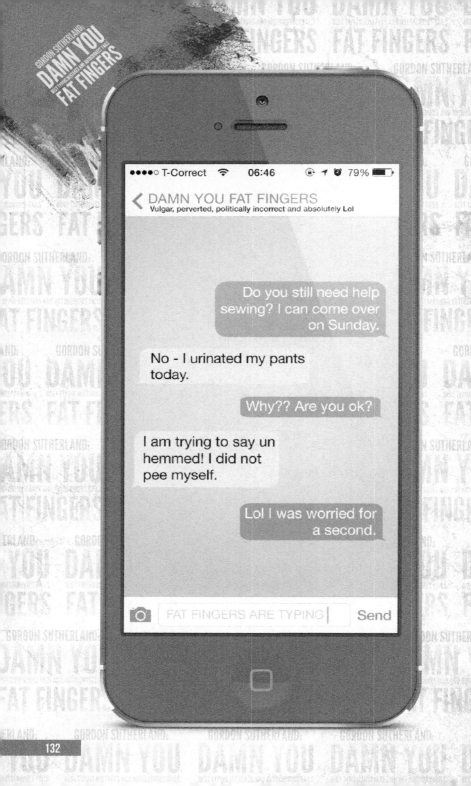

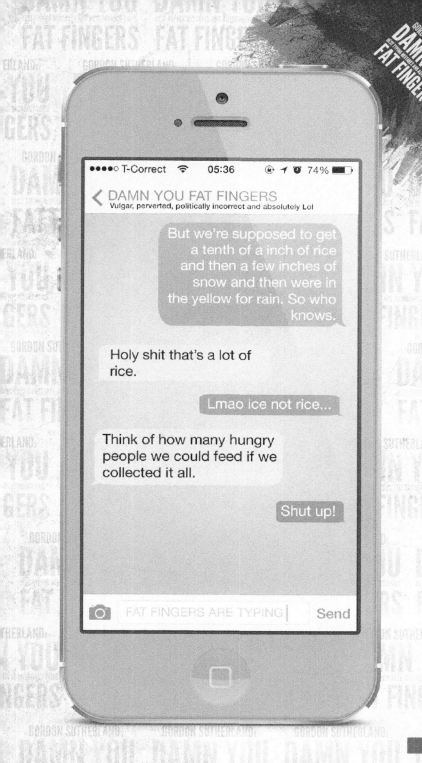

●●●●○ T-Correct 📶 05:36 📍 ✈ ⏱ 74% 🔋

‹ DAMN YOU FAT FINGERS
Vulgar, perverted, politically incorrect and absolutely Lol

> But we're supposed to get a tenth of a inch of rice and then a few inches of snow and then were in the yellow for rain. So who knows.

Holy shit that's a lot of rice.

> Lmao ice not rice...

Think of how many hungry people we could feed if we collected it all.

> Shut up!

📷 | FAT FINGERS ARE TYPING | Send

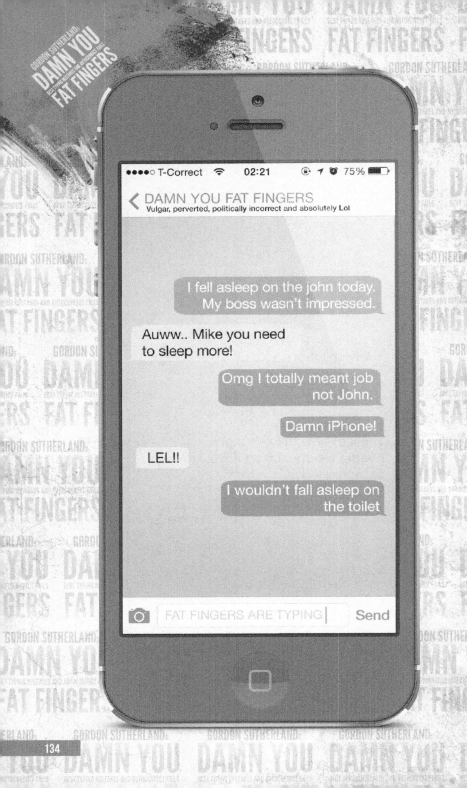

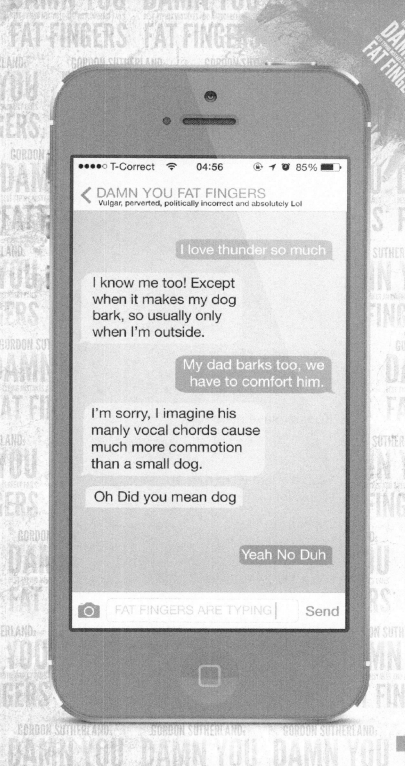

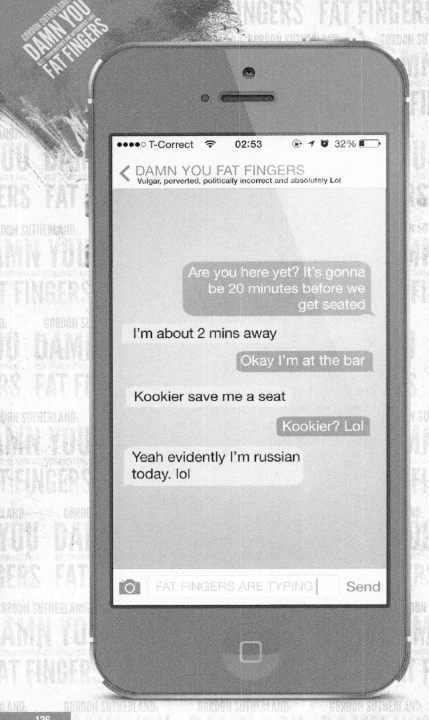

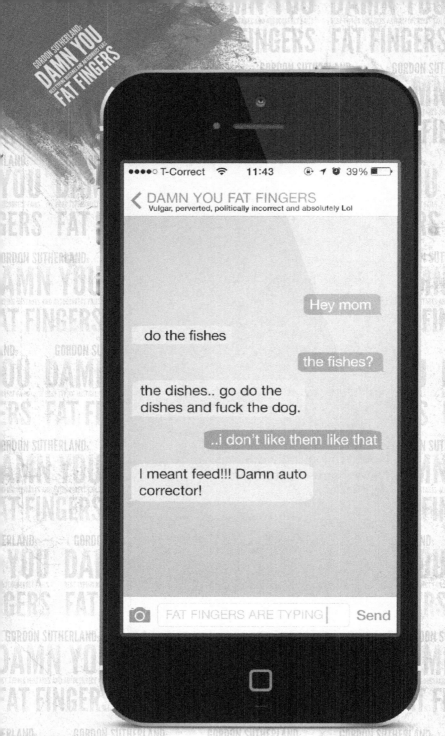

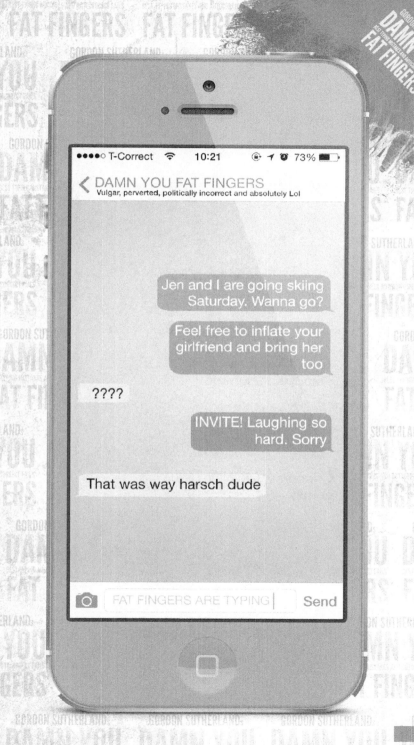

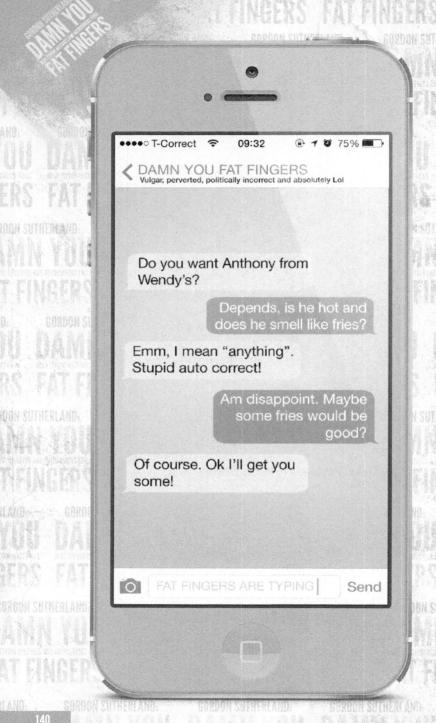

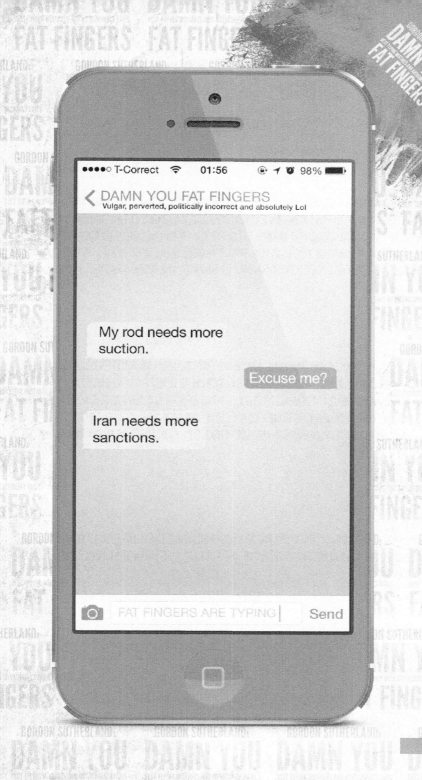

# Urban Dictionary

## LEL

UNLIKE WHAT MANY PEOPLE THINK LEL IS NOT AN ACRONYM IN THE SAME FASHION THAT LOL IS (IT DOES NOT MEAN LAUGHING EXTREMELY LOUD, LAUGHING EXTRA LOUD OR SIMILAR). LEL (AND VARIATIONS INCLUDING LAL) RESULTED FROM THE USE OF RANDOM VOWELS SUBSTITUTED IN PLACE OF THE 'O' IN LOL. THESE VOWELS WERE USED IN AN ATTEMPT TO BE DIFFERENT FROM THE MILLIONS OF INTERNET GAME FAGS. THE WORD HOWEVER, IN ESSENCE, STILL MEANS LOL.

## LOL

IT'S ORIGINAL DEFINITION WAS "LAUGHING OUT LOUD" (ALSO WRITTEN OCCASIONALLY AS "LOTS OF LAUGHS"), USED AS A BRIEF ACRONYM TO DENOTE GREAT AMUSEMENT IN CHAT CONVERSATIONS. NOW, IT IS OVERUSED TO THE POINT WHERE NOBODY LAUGHS OUT LOUD WHEN THEY SAY IT. IN FACT, THEY PROBABLY DON'T EVEN GIVE A SHIT ABOUT WHAT YOU JUST WROTE. MORE ACCURATELY, THE ACRONYM "LOL" SHOULD BE REDEFINED AS "LACK OF LAUGHTER."

## LMAO

"LAUGHING MY ASS OFF". USED ONLINE TO SHOW YOU FIND SOMETHING REALLY FUNNY OR ARE LAUGHING AT IT ALOT. STARTING TO BE USED IN REAL LIFE WHEN THEY FIND SOMETHING "EL-EM-AE-OH!".

## LMFAO

LAUGHING MY FUCKING ASS OFF. A TERM USED WHEN YOU ARE IN TEARS FROM LAUGHTER. USED MOSTLY ON INSTANT MESSAGING.

## HAHA

SHORT QUICK WAY OF LETTING SOMEBODY KNOW YOU ARE LAUGHING, MOST LIKELY AT THEM.

## OMG

NET-CENTRIC ABBREVIATION FOR THE POPULAR EXCLAMATION "OH MY GOD!" (GENERALLY USED IN CONVERSATIONS TO EXCLAIM SURPRISE OR DISGUST).

## WOW

AN INTERJECTION USED TO EXPRESS AMAZEMENT.
"WOW, THAT'S A BIG HOUSE!"

## OO

CONFUSED, STUNNED, OR WEIRDED OUT.
OO WHAT DO YOU MEAN?
OO WHAT IS THAT?!
OO WHOA WTF

## DUH

A WORD PEOPLE USE WHEN THE OBVIOUS IS STATED.

## WTF

WTF USUALLY REFERS TO 'WHAT THE FUCK'. IT CAN BE USED AS A QUESTION, AN EXCLAMATION, AND MANY OTHER USES. IT IS COMMONLY USED IN INTERNET CHATROOMS WHERE SWEARING IS CENSORED.

THE 'W' CAN BE USED AS WHAT, WHERE, WHO OR WHEN, FOLLOWING BY THE 'TF' WHICH IS ALWAYS 'THE FUCK'

WTF IS USUALLY USED WITH DUDE OR MATE
EXAMPLE 1: WTF JUST HAPPENED HERE?
EXAMPLE 2: DUDE, WTF!
EXAMPLE 3: WTF DID THAT?

# THANKS YOU

If autocorrect embarrassed you or pissed you off, we want to know about it! Take a screen shot of the incident with your iPhone (by pressing the sleep button at the top of the iPhone and the circular home button at the same time) and send it to us via the email below. If you get published in our next book you get a free copy of it. We'll be announcing our next book in Autumn 2015.

If you liked that book, you might leave a review at Amazon. We really appreciate that.

Have a nice time ;)

Damn You Fat Fingers
damnyoufatfingers@gmail.com

Made in the USA
Coppell, TX
21 December 2022